BANJO PATERSON'S PEOPLE

BANJO PATERSON'S PEOPLE

Selected Poems and Prose by A. B. Paterson *Illustrations by Dorothy Gauvin*

GP

HERITAGE GALLERY PRINTING

This edition published in 1996 by
Heritage Gallery Printing (BN 552 8677)
10 Crest Close, Bayview Heights, Cairns
Queensland 4870, Australia

This book is copyright.
Apart from any fair dealing for the purposes of private study,
research, criticism or review, as permitted under the Copyright
Act, no part may be reproduced by any process without written
permission. Inquiries should be addressed to the publisher.

Copyright © Dorothy Gauvin, 1987, 1996

National Library of Australia
Cataloguing-in-publication data

Paterson, A.B. (Andrew Barton), 1864-1941
  Banjo Paterson's people
  ISBN 0 646 26749 3
  1. Gauvin, Dorothy. 11. Title

Cover painting by Dorothy Gauvin

Produced by Mandarin Offset in Hong Kong
Printed in China

CONTENTS

INTRODUCTIONS
A. B. Paterson 1   *Dorothy Gauvin* 3

THE MAN FROM IRONBARK 6   A BUNCH OF ROSES 10

CLANCY OF THE OVERFLOW 12   SONG OF THE WHEAT 14

THE ALL RIGHT 'UN 16   HOW GILBERT DIED 18

THE GEEBUNG POLO CLUB 20   HOW M'GINNIS WENT MISSING 22

FROM IN PUSH SOCIETY 24   JIM CAREW 30

OUR NEW HORSE 32   AN IDYLL OF DANDALOO 36

TAR AND FEATHERS 38   SALTBUSH BILL 40   A BUSHMAN'S SONG 44

THE CITY OF DREADFUL THIRST 46   T.Y.S.O.N. 48

A DREAM OF THE MELBOURNE CUP 50   PIONEERS 52

THE RIDERS IN THE STAND 54   IN THE DROVING DAYS 56

WHEN DACEY RODE THE MULE 58   WITH THE CATTLE 60

THE WILD CATTLE from *An Outback Marriage* 64

SONG OF THE ARTESIAN WATER 70   SONG OF THE FUTURE 72

OLD PARDON, THE SON OF REPRIEVE 75

BANJO PATERSON'S PEOPLE

THE MAN FROM IRONBARK

DECEMBER 1892

It was the man from Ironbark who struck the Sydney town,
He wandered over street and park, he wandered up and down.
He loitered here, he loitered there, till he was like to drop,
Until at last in sheer despair he sought a barber's shop.
"'Ere! shave my beard and whiskers off, I'll be a man of mark,
I'll go and do the Sydney toff up home in Ironbark."

The barber man was small and flash, as barbers mostly are,
He wore a strike-your-fancy sash, he smoked a huge cigar;
He was a humorist of note and keen at repartee,
He laid the odds and kept a "tote", whatever that may be,
And when he saw our friend arrive, he whispered, "Here's a lark!
Just watch me catch him all alive, this man from Ironbark."

There were some gilded youths that sat along the barber's wall.
Their eyes were dull, their heads were flat, they had no brains at all;
To them the barber passed the wink, his dexter eyelid shut,
"I'll make this bloomin' yokel think his bloomin' throat is cut."
And as he soaped and rubbed it in he made a rude remark:
"I s'pose the flats is pretty green up there in Ironbark."

A grunt was all reply he got; he shaved the bushman's chin,
Then made the water boiling hot and dipped the razor in.
He raised his hand, his brow grew black, he paused awhile to gloat,
Then slashed the red-hot razor-back across his victim's throat;
Upon the newly-shaven skin it made a livid mark—
No doubt it fairly took him in—the man from Ironbark.

He fetched a wild up-country yell might wake the dead to hear,
And though his throat, he knew full well, was cut from ear to ear,
He struggled gamely to his feet, and faced the murd'rous foe:
"You've done for me! you dog, I'm beat! one hit before I go!
I only wish I had a knife, you blessed murdering shark!
But you'll remember all your life the man from Ironbark."

He lifted up his hairy paw, with one tremendous clout
He landed on the barber's jaw, and knocked the barber out.

He set to work with nail and tooth, he made the place a wreck;
He grabbed the nearest gilded youth, and tried to break his neck.
And all the while his throat he held to save his vital spark,
And "Murder! Bloody murder!" yelled the man from Ironbark.

IN THE BIG SMOKE

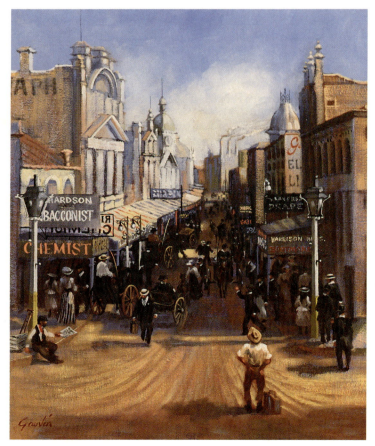

BANJO PATERSON'S PEOPLE

CONTENTS

Introductions
A. B. Paterson 1   *Dorothy Gauvin* 3

The Man from Ironbark 6   A Bunch of Roses 10

Clancy of The Overflow 12   Song of the Wheat 14

The All Right 'Un 16   How Gilbert Died 18

The Geebung Polo Club 20   How M'Ginnis Went Missing 22

From In Push Society 24   Jim Carew 30

Our New Horse 32   An Idyll of Dandaloo 36

Tar and Feathers 38   Saltbush Bill 40   A Bushman's Song 44

The City of Dreadful Thirst 46   T.Y.S.O.N. 48

A Dream of the Melbourne Cup 50   Pioneers 52

The Riders in the Stand 54   In the Droving Days 56

When Dacey Rode the Mule 58   With the Cattle 60

The Wild Cattle from *An Outback Marriage* 64

Song of the Artesian Water 70   Song of the Future 72

Old pardon, the Son of Reprieve 75

BANJO PATERSON'S PEOPLE

BANJO PATERSON'S PEOPLE

A. B. PATERSON

In a writing career that spanned over 50 years, Andrew Barton Paterson established himself as Australia's best-loved poet. His first contribution to the *Bulletin* was made (anonymously) when he was 21; he was still working as a freelance writer until just before his death at the age of 76. Paterson's most prolific period was during his 20s and 30s, when he produced many of the timeless pieces included in this collection.

Born in 1864 near Orange, New South Wales, young "Barty" Paterson had a fairly lonely youth. His only brother was 12 years his junior, and Paterson saw little of his father who was struggling to maintain two properties. When both these ventures failed, the family bought a station called Illalong, near Yass, but that too failed and the property was sold. The purchaser, however, agreed to employ Paterson's father to manage Illalong and he spent the rest of his life as a station manager.

When his father died in 1889, Paterson became the head of the household. His mother and five sisters joined him in Sydney where he was working as a clerk in a solicitor's office. Paterson was briefly in partnership with another lawyer, but in 1900 turned his back on a career in law and from that time on earned his income as a freelance journalist.

The first of Paterson's ballads to attract significant attention was "Old Pardon, the Son of Reprieve", published in the *Bulletin* in 1888 under the pseudonym "the Banjo", which was the name of one of his favourite horses. It was not until 1895, when Angus & Robertson published *The Man from Snowy River and Other Verses*, that "the Banjo's" true identity was revealed.

Unlike many of the *Bulletin* bohemians the life of a philanderer was unappealing to Paterson. At the age of 39 he married Alice Walker, an accomplished horserider and athlete who shared many of his interests. It was to be a happy and enduring marriage.

Although Paterson is best remembered as a poet, he was also a well-respected journalist and editor. He worked in a number of different areas, from war correspondent in South Africa during the Boer War to editor of the *Sportsman*. Paterson also spent some years as editor of the *Evening News*, a Sydney afternoon newspaper. He seems to have been torn between his enjoyment of the life of a Sydney writer and his love of the Australian bush. In 1908 Paterson moved to a property on the fringes of Snowy River country with his wife and two children, then later took over a wheat farm at Grenfell. From these ventures he returned to the city and his work as a journalist.

Amidst the boisterous camaraderie of Sydney's literary world, Paterson stood apart. As a young man he was quite shy, a country lad learning how to fit into city life. Although he is often portrayed as handsome and self-assured, he was surprisingly modest about his own literary endeavours. He once described "The Man From Snowy River" as "a jingle which has outlasted much better work", and dismissed "Waltzing Matilda" as "old junk".

Paterson was indeed a good-looking man, as Norman Lindsay's description of him at the height of his popularity indicates:

> . . . *It is rare that a superior spirit is given a superior casing, but Paterson had it. A tall man with a finely built, muscular body, moving with the ease of perfectly co-ordinated reflexes. Black hair, dark eyes, a long, finely articulated nose, an ironic mouth, a dark pigmentation of skin . . . His eyes, as eyes must be, were his most distinctive feature, slightly hooded, with a glance that looked beyond one as he talked . . .*

Paterson's remarkable ability to depict the mannerisms of the bush workers and his evocation of the Australian landscape enabled him to capture the hearts of his readers. With Paterson, the underdog stole the show: the shearer, the drover, the bushranger, all took pride of place in the Banjo's work. The resourceful and defiant Australians that have been immortalised in Paterson's poetry and prose are now seen as symbols of the nation's character.

BANJO PATERSON'S PEOPLE

BANJO PATERSON'S PEOPLE

DOROTHY GAUVIN

Dorothy Gauvin was seven years old when she told her father that she would be an artist. Twenty-six years were to pass before she was able to make that determination a reality. During that time, she worked for five years as a display artist before marrying Carl Wellington (now a successful businessman), brought up their son Paul (now working in partnership with his father) and won a 15-year battle with the crippling disease, rheumatoid arthritis. The painter now says: "Looking back, there's actually a sense of thankfulness for all those 'delays'. Because of them, by the time I finally got started, at least I had something to say."

That "something to say" is always the first priority for Gauvin, who believes that, no matter how cleverly or beautifully made, a work of art requires meaningful content or it remains mere decoration. This philosophy finds its best expression in her current series of paintings which draws its inspiration from the writings of A. B. (Banjo) Paterson.

Gauvin was born in Winton, western Queensland, not far from where Paterson wrote "Waltzing Matilda". The influence of the bush continued to run through her life as she grew up listening to her father's tales of his early life as a stockman on a cattle station in the remote Channel Country of Queensland. She taped her father's recollections as reference material when she began work on her first major series. These paintings depicted ageing bush characters reviewing their lives, in a style which even then was a precursor of her "montage" effects now being fully developed in the second series of *Banjo Paterson's People*. The early paintings appeared in the group exhibitions held at Surfers Paradise and Brisbane in 1976 and 1977, in which Gauvin was invited to show with such luminaries as Hugh Sawrey and Patrick Kilvington.

In that year, Gauvin won first prize in the "Traditional" section of the Garden City Art Prize. This led to her being offered her first solo show in 1978, again in Brisbane, which attracted both critical and public favour. The success of this show brought many portrait commissions, including one for Queensland's Parliament House. Due to the progression of her illness, it was not until 1980 that the artist mounted her next solo exhibition, in Cairns. This was followed by solo shows in Brisbane in 1981, and in 1982 she was awarded first prize for the "People in Pubs" section of the Castlemaine-Perkins Art Prize. In that year, her exhibition entitled "Women Convicts of Eagle Farm", imaginatively based on the sparse reference material available, was completely sold out within the first two hours of its opening night in Brisbane.

In 1983, conclusive evidence was finally accepted that the loss of all central vision in one of Gauvin's eyes was untreatable, and that the other eye might be at risk also. So Dorothy planned a trip to Europe to see for herself those paintings of the masters she'd grown up revering. This extensive tour, carried out in 1984, gave the painter a renewed determination to devote her art to expressing her view of her own country and the values on which its society was built. Ross Deegan, a long-time friend and fellow Paterson enthusiast, urged Gauvin to take the writings of Banjo Paterson as the springboard for her imagination. It was Rosamund Campbell who first kindly suggested that the paintings be collected in a new edition of her grandfather's work.

Ross and other friends supplied stock and military saddles, costumes and other accoutrements used in the paintings. Soon a steady stream of props began to arrive at the studio, among them the authentic old cutthroat razor and leather strops seen in "The Man from Ironbark" paintings. Family, friends and the occasional innocent bystander were roped in to model for the characters. When the paintings needed a large cast, some hilarious scenes were staged, any shyness being treated with liberal doses of the amber fluid while the artist got busy with sketchbook and camera. Even the family cat got into the act, and into one of the paintings.

About the paintings, Gauvin says:

Wherever possible, I've tried for something a little different in interpreting these famous poems. In "The Last Race" I wanted to

BANJO PATERSON'S PEOPLE

show that indeed the race has just been run, without painting the least suggestion of the horses. Most of the characters, I think, explain themselves, but if you notice the angle of the young woman's handmirror, you'll realise she's not looking at her own reflection, but is checking out prospects amongst the winning punters for a big night out on the town.

Like so many other Australian painters, I wanted to have a go at "The Geebung Polo Club". But was there any way I could avoid the usual scene of the melee on the playing field? That "they even brought their valets just to give their boots a rub" really tickled my fancy; "The Captains Meet", featuring a tin of good old Nugget shoe polish, is the result.

In "Dandaloo", nothing moves except the old woman leading her house cow back for milking, the lazy trickle of smoke from the chimneys, and the flicking of the horses' tails as they wait patiently at the hitching rail. Like many of its ilk, the pub has "grown like Topsy", the central core being added on to as the need arose, with whatever materials came to hand, while the imposing facade testifies to long-abandoned dreams of prosperity. On looking into the painting, you'll notice that an ironical triangle is formed connecting the church in the distance with the pub and the undertakers, two doors down.

"The Jobless Jackaroo" came within a whisker of destruction, so unhappy was I with it at one stage. Unhappy! I was pacing up and down the studio muttering through gritted teeth. After getting his tail trodden on a few times, the cat decamped in disgust and I shoved the half-finished painting in the storage racks, vowing it'd go to the incinerator. The sky was then blue and bland, the stockman also. Where was the atmosphere, the mood, the story? It had to go. I flung out of the studio and down into the small belt of rainforest behind our house. Sitting there in the dappled light, I began to rethink what I was trying to say with this painting, and slowly it came. No, it wasn't the work-shy shiftless bloke I'd first seen in "A Bushman's Song". The man I wanted was one who valued his freedom and his pride above any rules or conventions and was prepared to pay the price. So, my man has just met up with the Overlanders, bringing a mob down from Queensland. But the Boss can't give him a job, so he sells them his pack- and saddle-horses for cash to keep him going till he finds temporary work in the town. He hangs on to his stock saddle though, because as soon as things look up again, he'll be back droving too.

Since Paterson hadn't specified the locale for "The City of Dreadful Thirst", I figured this was a chance to introduce a female character, one I remembered Dad telling me about. Isobel Robinson, widely known outback as "the Eulo Queen", is perhaps thinly disguised as "the Opal Queen" in Paterson's novel, An Outback Marriage. It seems this lady, claiming an aristocratic lineage, arrived in Australia already widowed more than once, and settled at Eulo, then a tiny staging point for the western Cobb & Co. run. Here she set up in business selling grog to the passing shearers and opal gougers, often encouraging the latter to pay her in stones when the cash ran out. In time she owned most of the town, including the largest and most notorious gambling establishment in the inland. It's in reference to this that I used a gaming table in the foreground of the painting. Though described as having a "fine and buxom figure", I was unable to discover her colouring, but felt sure she'd sport a mane of brassy red-blonde hair. So when I'd settled on a magnificently well-endowed friend as the model, the only change I made was to her own short cap of black hair. The painting shows the moment when, having told his shaggy dog story, the man from Narromine sets down the now empty pint glass he'd won, while the squatter toasts him. That beer foam on the glass was a challenge in itself, and I wasted several perfectly good cans of Carl's favourite in a futile effort to keep the froth from melting away in the tropical heat before I could paint it. Then I recalled a trick my mother used in a similar circumstance. While demonstrating cookery on her television programme, she'd sometimes find whipped cream decorations melting under the hot lights and would then substitute shaving foam. So—a shot of foam, a little water, swill it around

BANJO PATERSON'S PEOPLE

the glass, and the resultant "beer foam" lasted a good 20 minutes, enough time to get it down convincingly on the canvas.

"The Wheat Farmers" forms the bridge between the classical style of the first series and the development of the second series. Here the background landscape comes from my memories of the years when my family lived at Toowoomba on the great wheat belt of Queensland's Darling Downs. A gentleman viewing the finished work protested that these characters looked "too European". When I laughed and asked him where he thought the early pioneers had come from, he scratched his head and then said, "Oh yeah, that's right! You tend to forget that. I s'pose if you'd put 'em in shorts or a bush hat they'd look typically Aussie, eh?"

Since the *Banjo Paterson's People* series began, many of the works have been sold even before completion, bringing five-figure prices from numerous private and corporate collectors of Gauvin's work throughout Australia and in the USA.

Of A. B. Paterson, the artist says:

To me, in his writing (especially in his verse), Paterson gets to the very heart of what it means to be an Australian. To do that as he does, with so much humour and optimism, takes far more courage than to join all the moaners and knockers. It's a bonus that we can like and respect the man himself, for his exemplary life reflects a very fine mind and character. His writings offer a seemingly endless wellspring of inspiration, and I would like to think he might have enjoyed these paintings.

Dimensions of Paintings

"The Man from Ironbark", **In the Big Smoke** — 51 cm x 66 cm
    The Barber's Boy and the Bludgers — 76 cm x 66 cm
    The Man from Ironbark No. 1 — 91.5 cm x 122 cm
    The Man from Ironbark No. 2 — 91.5 cm x 122 cm
"A Bunch of Roses", **White Roses** — 76 cm x 91.5 cm
"Clancy of the Overflow", **Clancy** — 71 cm x 76cm
"Song of the Wheat", **The Wheat Farmers** — 91.5 cm x 122 cm
"The All Right 'Un", **The All Right 'Un** — 56 cm x 71 cm
"How Gilbert Died", **The Outlaws** — 56 cm x 76 cm
"The Geebung Polo Club", **The Captains Meet** — 61 cm x 91.5 cm
"How M'Ginnis Went Missing", **M'Ginnis and the Bottle** — 66 cm x 76 cm
"In Push Society", **Gentleman Jim and the Larrikins** — 91.5 cm x 122 cm
"Jim Carew", **Gentleman Jim No. 2** — 76 cm x 91.5 cm
"Our New Horse", **The Station Hands' Quarters** — 71 cm x 91.5 cm
    Springtime on the Station — 51 cm x 66 cm
"An Idyll of Dandaloo", **Dandaloo** — 51 cm x 66 cm
"Tar and Feathers", **The Showman** — 76 cm x 91.5 cm

"Saltbush Bill", **Saltbush Bill** — 51 cm x 71 cm
    Saltbush Bill's Inquest — 61 cm x 91.5 cm
"A Bushman's Song", **The Jobless Jackaroo** — 91.5 cm x 122 cm
"The City of Dreadful Thirst", **In the Eulo Queen's Pub** — 91.5 cm x 122 cm
"T.Y.S.O.N.", **Country Town** — 56 cm x 61 cm
"A Dream of the Melbourne Cup", **Melbourne Cup Bookies** — 61 cm x 91.5 cm
"Pioneers", **Going Bush Again** — 61 cm x 91.5 cm
"The Riders in the Stand", **The Last Race** — 91.5 cm x 122 cm
"In the Droving Days", **At Auction** — 61 cm x 91.5 cm
"When Dacey Rode the Mule", **Dacey and the Mule** — 71 cm x 91.5 cm
"With the Cattle", **The Stockmen** — 51 cm x 66 cm
    The Overlanders — 75 cm x 112 cm
"The Wild Cattle", **Turning the Wild Cattle** — 41 cm x 51 cm
"Song of the Artesian Water", **Drilling for Water** — 91.5 cm x 122 cm
"Song of the Future", **Australia Past and Future** — 91.5 cm x 122 cm
"Old Pardon, the Son of Reprieve", **The Hereafter Racecourse** — 30.5 cm x 46 cm

BANJO PATERSON'S PEOPLE

THE MAN FROM IRONBARK

DECEMBER 1892

It was the man from Ironbark who struck the Sydney town,
He wandered over street and park, he wandered up and down.
He loitered here, he loitered there, till he was like to drop,
Until at last in sheer despair he sought a barber's shop.
"'Ere! shave my beard and whiskers off, I'll be a man of mark,
I'll go and do the Sydney toff up home in Ironbark."

The barber man was small and flash, as barbers mostly are,
He wore a strike-your-fancy sash, he smoked a huge cigar;
He was a humorist of note and keen at repartee,
He laid the odds and kept a "tote", whatever that may be,
And when he saw our friend arrive, he whispered, "Here's a lark!
Just watch me catch him all alive, this man from Ironbark."

There were some gilded youths that sat along the barber's wall.
Their eyes were dull, their heads were flat, they had no brains at all;
To them the barber passed the wink, his dexter eyelid shut,
"I'll make this bloomin' yokel think his bloomin' throat is cut."
And as he soaped and rubbed it in he made a rude remark:
"I s'pose the flats is pretty green up there in Ironbark."

A grunt was all reply he got; he shaved the bushman's chin,
Then made the water boiling hot and dipped the razor in.
He raised his hand, his brow grew black, he paused awhile to gloat,
Then slashed the red-hot razor-back across his victim's throat;
Upon the newly-shaven skin it made a livid mark—
No doubt it fairly took him in—the man from Ironbark.

He fetched a wild up-country yell might wake the dead to hear,
And though his throat, he knew full well, was cut from ear to ear,
He struggled gamely to his feet, and faced the murd'rous foe:
"You've done for me! you dog, I'm beat! one hit before I go!
I only wish I had a knife, you blessed murdering shark!
But you'll remember all your life the man from Ironbark."

He lifted up his hairy paw, with one tremendous clout
He landed on the barber's jaw, and knocked the barber out.

He set to work with nail and tooth, he made the place a wreck;
He grabbed the nearest gilded youth, and tried to break his neck.
And all the while his throat he held to save his vital spark,
And "Murder! Bloody murder!" yelled the man from Ironbark.

IN THE BIG SMOKE

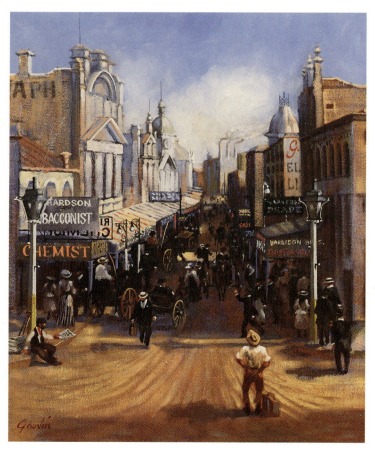

BANJO PATERSON'S PEOPLE

THE BARBER'S BOY AND THE BLUDGERS

A peeler man who heard the din came in to see the show;
He tried to run the bushman in, but he refused to go.
And when at last the barber spoke, and said "'Twas all in fun—
'Twas just a little harmless joke, a trifle overdone."
"A joke!" he cried, "By George, that's fine; a lively sort of lark;
I'd like to catch that murdering swine some night in Ironbark."

And now while round the shearing floor the list'ning shearers gape,
He tells the story o'er and o'er, and brags of his escape.
"Them barber chaps what keeps a tote, By George, I've had enough,
One tried to cut my bloomin' throat, but thank the Lord it's tough."
And whether he's believed or no, there's one thing to remark,
That flowing beards are all the go way up in Ironbark.

BANJO PATERSON'S PEOPLE

THE MAN FROM IRONBARK NO. 1

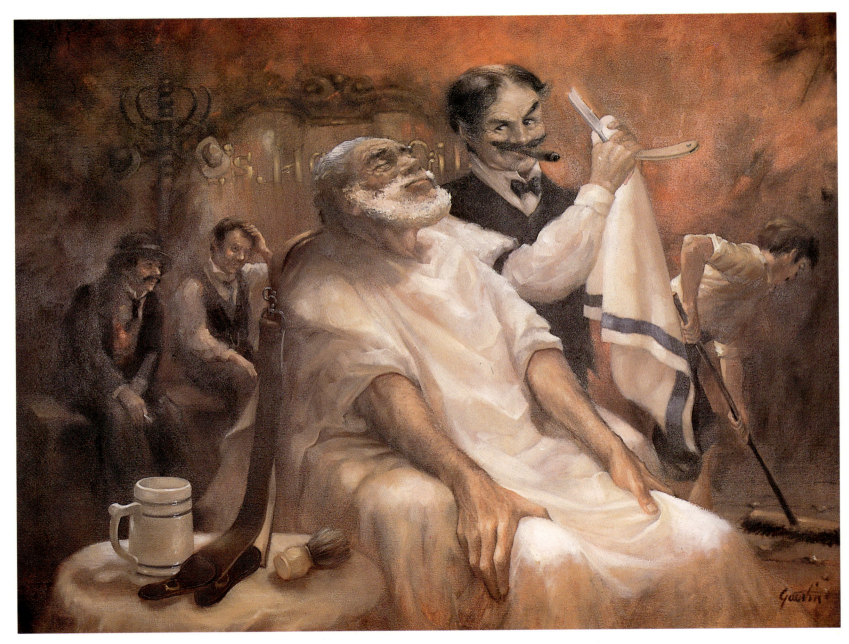

BANJO PATERSON'S PEOPLE

THE MAN FROM IRONBARK NO. 2

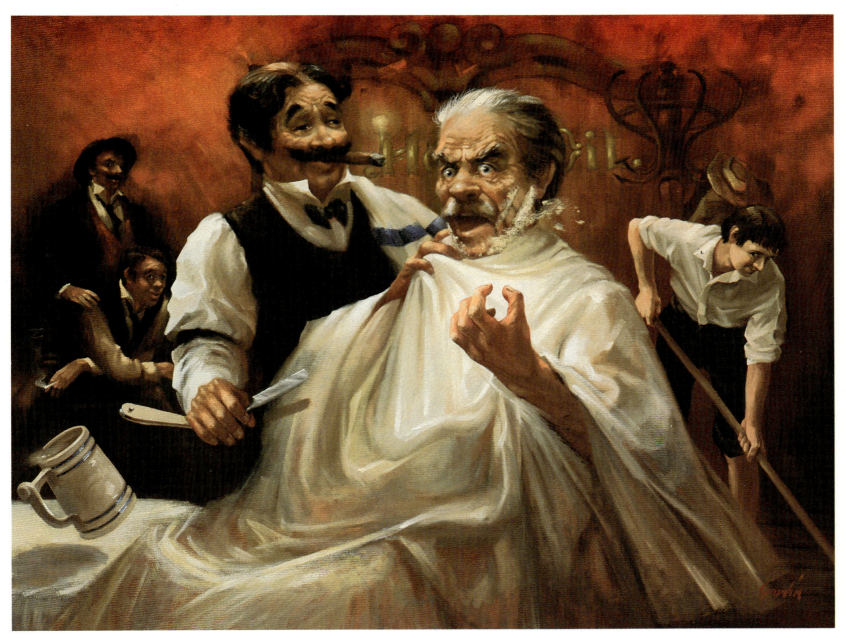

BANJO PATERSON'S PEOPLE

A BUNCH OF ROSES

19 MAY 1894

Roses ruddy and roses white,
    What are the joys that my heart discloses?
Sitting alone in the faded light
Memories come to me here to-night
    With the wonderful scent of the big red roses.

Memories come as the daylight fades
    Down on the hearth where the firelight dozes;
Flicker and flutter the lights and shades,
And I see the face of a queen of maids
    Whose memory comes with the scent of roses.

Visions arise of a scene of mirth,
    And a ballroom belle that superbly poses—
A queenly woman of queenly worth,
And I am the happiest man on earth
    With a single flower from a bunch of roses.

Only her memory lives tonight—
    God in His wisdom her young life closes;
Over her grave may the turf be light,
Cover her coffin with roses white—
    She was always fond of the big white roses.

Such are the visions that fade away—
    Man proposes and God disposes;
Look in the glass and I see to-day
Only an old man, worn and grey,
    Bending his head to a bunch of roses.

WHITE ROSES

BANJO PATERSON'S PEOPLE

CLANCY OF THE OVERFLOW

DECEMBER 1889

I had written him a letter which I had, for want of better
    Knowledge, sent to where I met him down the Lachlan, years ago,
He was shearing when I knew him, so I sent the letter to him,
    Just "on spec", addressed as follows: "Clancy, of The Overflow".

And an answer came directed in a writing unexpected,
    (And I think the same was written with a thumbnail dipped in tar)
'Twas his shearing mate who wrote it, and *verbatim* I will quote it:
    "Clancy's gone to Queensland droving, and we don't know where he are."

In my wild erratic fancy visions come to me of Clancy
    Gone a-droving "down the Cooper" where the western drovers go;
As the stock are slowly stringing, Clancy rides behind them singing,
    For the drover's life has pleasures that the townsfolk never know.

And the bush hath friends to meet him, and their kindly voices greet him
    In the murmur of the breezes and the river on its bars,
And he sees the vision splendid of the sunlit plains extended,
    And at night the wondrous glory of the everlasting stars.

I am sitting in my dingy little office, where a stingy
    Ray of sunlight struggles feebly down between the houses tall,
And the foetid air and gritty of the dusty, dirty city
    Through the open window floating, spreads its foulness over all.

And in place of lowing cattle, I can hear the fiendish rattle
    Of the tramways and the buses making hurry down the street,
And the language uninviting of the gutter children fighting,
    Comes fitfully and faintly through the ceaseless tramp of feet.

And the hurrying people daunt me, and their pallid faces haunt me
    As they shoulder one another in their rush and nervous haste,
With their eager eyes and greedy, and their stunted forms and weedy,
    For townsfolk have no time to grow, they have no time to waste.

And I somehow rather fancy that I'd like to change with Clancy,
    Like to take a turn at droving where the seasons come and go,
While he faced the round eternal of the cashbook and the journal—
    But I doubt he'd suit the office, Clancy of "The Overflow".

CLANCY

BANJO PATERSON'S PEOPLE

SONG OF THE WHEAT
NOVEMBER 1914

We have sung the song of the droving days,
   Of the march of the travelling sheep;
By silent stages and lonely ways
   Thin, white battalions creep.
But the man who now by the land would thrive
   Must his spurs to a ploughshare beat.
Is there ever a man in the world alive
   To sing the song of the Wheat!

It's west by south of the Great Divide
   The grim grey plains run out,
Where the old flock masters lived and died
   In a ceaseless fight with drought.
Weary with waiting and hope deferred
   They were ready to own defeat,
Till at last they heard the master-word
   And the master-word was Wheat.

Yarran and Myall and Box and Pine—
   'Twas axe and fire for all;
They scarce could tarry to blaze the line
   Or wait for the trees to fall,
Ere the team was yoked and the gates flung wide,
   And the dust of the horses' feet
Rose up like a pillar of smoke to guide
   The wonderful march of Wheat.

Furrow by furrow, and fold by fold,
   The soil is turned on the plain;
Better than silver and better than gold
   Is the surface-mine of the grain.
Better than cattle and better than sheep
   In the fight with the drought and heat.
For a streak of stubbornness wide and deep
   Lies hid in a grain of Wheat.

When the stock is swept by the hand of fate,
   Deep down in his bed of clay,
The brave brown Wheat will lie and wait
   For the resurrection day;
Lie hid while the whole world thinks him dead;
   But the spring rain, soft and sweet,
Will over the steaming paddocks spread
   The first green flush of the Wheat.

Green and amber and gold it grows
   When the sun sinks late in the west
And the breeze sweeps over the rippling rows
   Where the quail and the skylark nest.
Mountain or river or shining star,
   There's never a sight can beat—
Away to the skyline stretching far—
   A sea of the ripening Wheat.

When the burning harvest sun sinks low,
   And the shadows stretch on the plain,
The roaring strippers come and go
   Like ships on a sea of grain;
Till the lurching, groaning waggons bear
   Their tale of the load complete.
Of the world's great work he has done his share
   Who has gathered a crop of wheat.

Princes and Potentates and Czars,
   They travel in regal state,
But old King Wheat has a thousand cars
   For his trip to the water-gate;
And his thousand steamships breast the tide
   And plough thro' the wind and sleet
To the lands where the teeming millions bide
   That say, "Thank God for Wheat!"

BANJO PATERSON'S PEOPLE

THE WHEAT FARMERS

BANJO PATERSON'S PEOPLE

THE ALL RIGHT 'UN

AUGUST 1893

He came from "further out",
That land of heat and drought
And dust and gravel.
He got a touch of sun,
And rested at the run
Until his cure was done,
And he could travel.

When spring had decked
 the plain,
He flitted off again
As flit the swallows.
And from that western land,
When many months were
 spanned,
A letter came to hand,
Which read as follows:

"Dear Sir, I take my pen
In hopes that all your men
And you are hearty.
You think that I've forgot
Your kindness, Mr Scott,
Oh, no, dear sir, I'm not
That sort of party.

"You sometimes bet, I know,
Well, now you'll have a show
The 'books' to frighten.
Up here at Wingadee
Young Billy Fife and me
We're training Strife, and he
Is a all right 'un.

"Just now we're running byes,
But, sir, first time he tries
I'll send you word of.
And running 'on the crook'
Their measures we have took,
It is the deadest hook
You ever heard of.

"So when we lets him go,
Why, then, I'll let you know,
And you can have a show
To put a mite on.
Now, sir, my leave I'll take,
Yours truly, William Blake.
P.S. Make no mistake,
He's a all right 'un."

By next week's *Riverine*
I saw my friend had been
A bit too cunning.
I read: "The racehorse Strife
And jockey William Fife
Disqualified for life —
Suspicious running."

But though they spoilt his game,
I reckon all the same
I fairly ought to claim
My friend a white 'un.
For though he wasn't straight,
His deeds would indicate
His heart at any rate
Was "a all right 'un".

THE ALL RIGHT 'UN

HOW GILBERT DIED

JUNE 1894

There's never a stone at the sleeper's head,
   There's never a fence beside,
And the wandering stock on the grave may tread
   Unnoticed and undenied,
But the smallest child on the Watershed
   Can tell you how Gilbert died.

For he rode at dusk, with his comrade Dunn
   To the hut at the Stockman's Ford,
In the waning light of the sinking sun
   They peered with a fierce accord.
They were outlaws both—and on each man's head
   Was a thousand pounds reward.

They had taken toll of the country round,
   And the troopers came behind
With a black that tracked like a human hound
   In the scrub and the ranges blind:
He could run the trail where a white man's eye
   No sign of a track could find.

He had hunted them out of the One Tree Hill
   And over the Old Man Plain,
But they wheeled their tracks with a wild beast's skill,
   And they made for the range again.
Then away to the hut where their grandsire dwelt,
   They rode with a loosened rein.

And their grandsire gave them a greeting bold:
   "Come in and rest in peace,
No safer place does the country hold—
   With the night pursuit must cease,
And we'll drink success to the roving boys,
   And to hell with the black police."

But they went to death when they entered there,
   In the hut at the Stockman's Ford,
For their grandsire's words were as false as fair—
   They were doomed to the hangman's cord.
He had sold them both to the black police
   For the sake of the big reward.

In the depth of night there are forms that glide
   As stealthy as serpents creep,
And around the hut where the outlaws hide
   They plant in the shadows deep,
And they wait till the first faint flush of dawn
   Shall waken their prey from sleep.

But Gilbert wakes while the night is dark—
   A restless sleeper, aye,
He has heard the sound of a sheepdog's bark,
   And his horse's warning neigh,
And he says to his mate, "There are hawks abroad,
   And it's time that we went away."

Their rifles stood at the stretcher head,
   Their bridles lay to hand,
They wakened the old man out of his bed,
   When they heard the sharp command:
"In the name of the Queen lay down your arms,
   Now, Dunn and Gilbert, stand!"

Then Gilbert reached for his rifle true
   That close at his hand he kept,
He pointed it straight at the voice and drew,
   But never a flash outleapt,
For the water ran from the rifle breach—
   It was drenched while the outlaws slept.

Then he dropped the piece with a bitter oath,
   And he turned to his comrade Dunn:
"We are sold," he said, "we are dead men both,
   But there may be a chance for one;
I'll stop and I'll fight with the pistol here,
   You take to your heels and run."

So Dunn crept out on his hands and knees
   In the dim, half-dawning light,
And he made his way to a patch of trees,
   And vanished among the night,
And the trackers hunted his tracks all day,
   But they never could trace his flight.

But Gilbert walked from the open door
   In a confident style and rash;
He heard at his side the rifles roar,
   And he heard the bullets crash.
But he laughed as he lifted his pistol-hand,
   And he fired at the rifle flash.

Then out of the shadows the troopers aimed
   At his voice and the pistol sound,
With the rifle flashes the darkness flamed,
   He staggered and spun around,
And they riddled his body with rifle balls
   As it lay on the blood-soaked ground.

There's never a stone at the sleeper's head
   There's never a fence beside,
And the wandering stock on the grave may tread
   Unnoticed and undenied,
But the smallest child on the Watershed
   Can tell you how Gilbert died.

THE OUTLAWS

BANJO PATERSON'S PEOPLE

THE GEEBUNG POLO CLUB

1893

It was somewhere up the country, in a land of rock and scrub,
That they formed an institution called the Geebung Polo Club.
They were long and wiry natives from the rugged mountainside,
And the horse was never saddled that the Geebungs couldn't ride;
But their style of playing polo was irregular and rash—
They had mighty little science, but a mighty lot of dash:
And they played on mountain ponies that were muscular and strong,
Though their coats were quite unpolished, and their manes and tails were long.
And they used to train those ponies wheeling cattle in the scrub:
They were demons, were the members of the Geebung Polo Club.

It was somewhere down the country, in a city's smoke and steam,
That a polo club existed, called the Cuff and Collar Team.
As a social institution 'twas a marvellous success,
For the members were distinguished by exclusiveness and dress.
They had natty little ponies that were nice, and smooth, and sleek,
For their cultivated owners only rode 'em once a week.
So they started up the country in pursuit of sport and fame,
For they meant to show the Geebungs how they ought to play the game;
And they took their valets with them—just to give their boots a rub
Ere they started operations on the Geebung Polo Club.

Now my readers can imagine how the contest ebbed and flowed,
When the Geebung boys got going it was time to clear the road;
And the game was so terrific that ere half the time was gone
A spectator's leg was broken—just from merely looking on.
For they waddied one another till the plain was strewn with dead,
While the score was kept so even that they neither got ahead.
And the Cuff and Collar captain, when he tumbled off to die,
Was the last surviving player—so the game was called a tie.

Then the captain of the Geebungs raised him slowly from the ground,
Though his wounds were mostly mortal, yet he fiercely gazed around;
There was no one to oppose him—all the rest were in a trance,
So he scrambled on his pony for his last expiring chance,
For he meant to make an effort to get victory to his side;
So he struck at goal—and missed it—then he tumbled off and died.

By the old Campaspe River, where the breezes shake the grass,
There's a row of little gravestones that the stockmen never pass,
For they bear a crude inscription saying, "Stranger, drop a tear,
For the Cuff and Collar players and the Geebung boys lie here."
And on misty moonlit evenings, while the dingoes howl around,
You can see their shadows flitting down that phantom polo ground;
You can hear the loud collisions as the flying players meet,
And the rattle of the mallets, and the rush of ponies' feet,
Till the terrified spectator rides like blazes to the pub—
He's been haunted by the spectres of the Geebung Polo Club.

THE CAPTAINS MEET

How M'Ginnis Went Missing

SEPTEMBER 1889

Let us cease our idle chatter,
   Let the tears bedew our cheek,
For a man from Tallangatta
   Has been missing for a week.

Where the roaring, flooded Murray
   Covered all the lower land,
There he started in a hurry,
   With a bottle in his hand.

And his fate is hid for ever,
   But the public seem to think
That he slumbered by the river,
   'Neath the influence of drink.

And they scarcely seem to wonder
   That the river, wide and deep,
Never woke him with its thunder,
   Never stirred him in his sleep.

As the crashing logs came sweeping,
   And their tumult filled the air,
Then M'Ginnis murmured, sleeping,
   "'Tis a wake in ould Kildare."

So the river rose and found him
   Sleeping softly by the stream,
And the cruel waters drowned him
   Ere he wakened from his dream.

And the blossom-tufted wattle,
   Blooming brightly on the lea
Saw M'Ginnis and the bottle
   Going drifting out to sea.

M'GINNIS AND THE BOTTLE

From In Push Society

THE PASSING of the evening afterwards is the only true test of a dinner's success. Many a good dinner, enlivened with wine and made brilliant with repartee, has died out in gloom. The guests have all said their best things during the meal, and nothing is left but to smoke moodily and look at the clock. Our heroes were not of that mettle. They meant to have some sort of fun, and the various amusements of Sydney were canvassed. It was unanimously voted too hot for the theatres, ditto for billiards. There were no supporters for a proposal to stop in the smoking-room and drink, and gambling in the card-rooms had no attractions on such a night. At last Gordon hit off a scent.

"What do you say," he drawled, "if we go and have a look at a dancing saloon—one of these larrikin dancing saloons?"

"I'd like it awfully," said one Englishman.

"Most interesting," said the other. "I've heard such a lot about the Australian larrikin. What they call a basher in England, isn't it? Eh, what? Sort of rough that lays for you with a pal and robs you, eh?"

The Bo'sun rang for cigars and liqueurs, and then answered the question. "Pretty much the same as a basher," he said, "but with a lot more science and dog-cunning about him. They go in gangs, and if you hit one of the gang, all the rest will 'deal with you', as they call it. If they have to wait a year to get you, they'll wait, and get you alone some night or other and set on to you. They jump on a man if they get him down, too. Oh, they're regular beauties."

"Rather roughish sort of Johnnies, eh?" said the Englishman. "But we might go and see the dancing—no harm in that."

Pinnock said he had to go back to his office; the globe-trotter didn't care about going out at night: and the Bo'sun tried to laugh the thing off. "You don't catch me going," he said. "There's nothing to be seen—just a lot of flash young rowdies dancing. You'll gape at them, and they'll gape at you, and you'll feel rather a pair of fools, and you'll come away. Better stop and have a rubber."

"If you dance with any of their woman, you get her particular fancy-man on to you, don't you?" asked Gordon. "It's years since I was at that sort of place myself."

The Bo'sun, who knew nothing about it, assumed the Sir Oracle at once.

"I don't suppose their women would dance with you if you paid 'em five shillings a step," he said. "There'd certainly be a fight if they did. Are you fond of fighting, Carew?"

"Not a bit," replied that worthy. "Never fight if you can help it. No chap with any sense ever does."

"That's like me," said Gordon. "I'd sooner run a mile than fight, any time. I'm like a rat if I'm cornered, but it takes a man with a stockwhip to corner me. I never start fighting till I'm done running. But we needn't get into a row. I vote we go. Will you come, Carew?"

"Oh, yes; I'd like to," said the Englishman. "I don't suppose we need get into a fight."

So, after many jeers from the Bo'sun, and promises to come back and tell him all about it, Carew and Gordon sallied forth, a pair of men as capable of looking after themselves as one would meet in a day's

GENTLEMAN JIM AND THE LARRIKINS

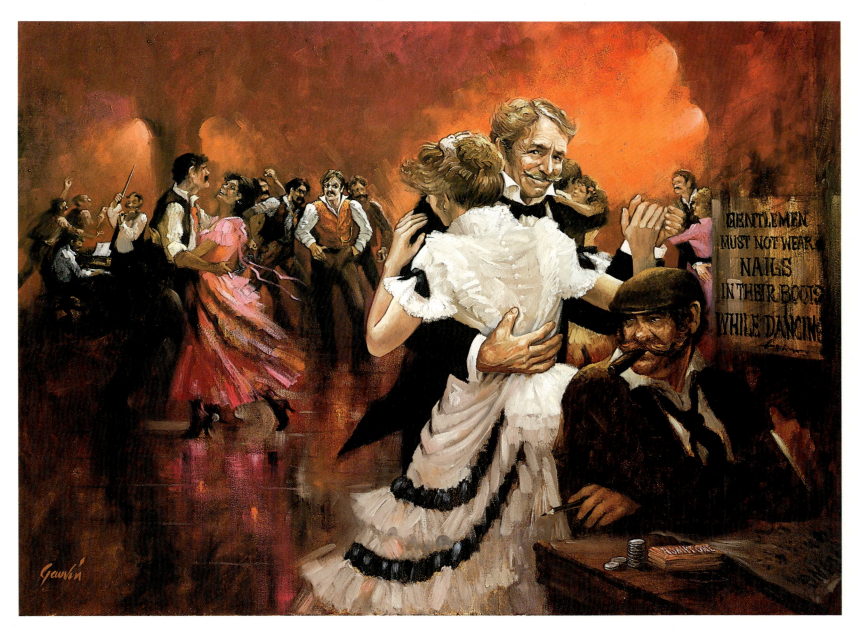

march. Stepping into the street they called a cab.

"Where to, sir?" asked the cabman.

"Nearest dancing saloon," said Gordon, briefly.

"Nearest darncin' saloon," said the cabman. "There ain't no parties tonight, sir; it's too 'ot."

"We're not expecting to drop into a ballroom without being asked, thank you," said Gordon. "We want to go to one of those saloons where you pay a shilling to go in. Some place where the larrikins go."

"Ho! is that it, sir?" said the cabman, with a grin. "Well, I'll take you to a noo place, most selectest place I know. Git up, 'orse." And off they rattled through the quiet streets, turning corners and crossing tramlines every fifty yards, apparently, and bumping against each other in the most fraternal manner.

Soon the cab pulled up in a narrow, ill-lit street, at the open door of a dingy house. Instructing the cabman to wait, they hustled upstairs, to be confronted at the top by a man who took a shilling from each, and then was not sure whether he would admit them. He didn't seem to like their form exactly, and muttered something to a by-stander as they went in. They saw a long, low room, brilliantly lighted by flaring gas jets. Down one side, on wooden forms, was seated a row of flashily dressed girls—larrikinesses on their native heath, barmaids from cheap, disreputable hotels, shop girls, factory girls—all sharp-faced and pert, young in years, but old in knowledge of evil. The demon of mischief peeped out of their quick-moving restless eyes. They had elaborate fringes, and their short dresses exhibited well-turned ankles and legs.

A large notice on the wall stated that "Gentlemen must not dance with nails in their boots. Gentlemen must not dance together."

"That blocks us," said Gordon, pointing to the notice. "Can't dance together, no matter how much we want to. Look at these fellows here."

Opposite the women sat or lounged a score or two of youths—wiry, hard-faced little fellows, for the most part, with scarcely a sizeable man amongst them. They were all clothed in "push" evening dress— black bell-bottomed pants, no waistcoat, very short black paget coat, white shirt with no collar, and a gaudy neckerchief round the bare throat. Their boots were marvels, very high in the heel and picked out with all sorts of colours down the sides. They looked "varminty" enough for anything; but the shifty eyes, low foreheads, and evil faces gave our two heroes a sense of disgust. The Englishman thought that all the stories he had heard of the Australian larrikin must be exaggerated, and that any man who was at all athletic could easily hold his own among such a poor-looking lot. The whole spectacle was disappointing. The most elaborately decorous order prevailed; no excitement or rough play was noticeable and their expedition seemed likely to be a failure.

The bushman stared down the room with far-seeing eyes, apparently looking at nothing, and contemplated the whole show with bored indifference.

"Nothing very dazzling about this," he said. "I'm afraid we can't show you anything very exciting here. Better go back to the club, eh?"

Just then the band (piano and violin) struck up a slow, laboured waltz, "Bid me goodbye and go," and each black-coated male, with languid self-possession, strolled across the room, seized a lady by the arm, jerked her to her feet without saying a syllable, and commenced to dance in slow, convulsive movements, making a great many revolutions for very little progress. Two or three girls were left sitting, as their partners were talking in a little knot at the far end of the room; one among them was conspicuously pretty, and she began to ogle Carew in a very pronounced way.

"There's one hasn't got a partner," said Gordon. "Good-looking Tottie, too. Go and ask her to dance. See what she says."

The Englishman hesitated for a second. "I don't like asking a perfect stranger to dance," he said.

"Go on," said Gordon, "it's all right. She'll like it."

Carew drew down his cuffs, squared his shoulders, assumed his most absolutely stolid drawing-room manner, and walked across the room, a gleaming vision of splendour in his immaculate evening dress.

"May I—er—have the pleasure of this dance?" he said, with elaborate politeness.

The girl giggled a little, but said nothing, then rose and took his arm.

As she did so, a youth among the talkers at the other end of the room looked round, and stared for a second. Then he moistened his fingers with his tongue, smoothed the hair on his temples, and with elbows held out from his sides, shoulders hunched up and under-jaw stuck well out, bore down on Carew and the girl, who were getting under way when he came up. Taking not the slightest notice of Carew, he touched the girl on the shoulder with a sharp peremptory tap, and brought their dance to a stop.

"'Ere," he said, in commanding tones. "'Oo are you darncin' with?"

"I'm darncin' with 'im," answered the girl, pertly, indicating the Englishman with a jerk of her head.

"Ho, you're darncin' with 'im, are you? 'E brought you 'ere, p'r'aps?"

"No, he didn't," she said.

"No," said he. "You know well enough 'e didn't."

While this conversation was going on, the Englishman maintained an attitude of dignified reserve, leaving it to the lady to decide who was to be the favoured man. At last he felt it was hardly right for an Oxford man, and a triple blue at that, to be discussed in this contemptuous way by a larrikin and his "donah", so he broke into the discussion, perhaps a little abruptly, but using his most polished style.

"I—ah—asked this lady to dance, and if she—er—would be kind enough to do me the honour," he said, "I—"

"Oh! you arst 'er to darnce? And what right 'ad you to arst 'er to darnce, you lop-eared rabbit?" interrupted the larrikin, raising his voice as he warmed to his subject. "I brought 'er 'ere. I paid the shillin'. Now then, you take your 'ook," he went on, pointing sternly to the door, and talking as he would to a disobedient dog. "Go on, now. Take your 'ook."

The Englishman said nothing, but his jaw set ominously. The girl giggled, delighted at being the centre

BANJO PATERSON'S PEOPLE

of so much observation. The band stopped playing, and the dancers crowded round. Word was passed down that it was a "toff darncin' with Nugget's donah", and from various parts of the room black-coated duplicates of Nugget hurried swiftly to the scene.

The doorkeeper turned to Gordon. "You'd best get your mate out o' this," he said. "These are the Rocks Push, and they'll deal with him all right."

"Deal with him, will they?" said Gordon, looking at the gesticulating Nugget. "They'll bite off more than they can chew if they interfere with him. This is just his form, a row like this. He's a bit of a champion in a rough-and-tumble, I believe."

"Is he?" said the doorkeeper, sardonically. 'Well, look 'ere, now, you take it from me, if there's a row Nugget will spread him out as flat as a newspaper. They've all been in the ring in their time, these coves. There's Nugget, and Ginger, and Brummy — all red 'ot. You get him away!"

Meanwhile the Englishman's ire was gradually rising. He was past the stage of considering whether it was worth while to have a fight over a factory girl in a shilling dancing saloon, and the desire for battle blazed up in his eyes. He turned and confronted Nugget.

"You go about your business," he said, dropping all the laboured politeness out of his tones. "If she likes to dance—"

He got no further. A shrill whistle rang through the room; a voice shouted, "Don't 'it 'im; 'ook 'im!" His arms were seized from behind and pinioned to his sides. The lights were turned out. Somebody in front hit him a terrific crack in the eye at the same moment that someone else administered a violent kick from the rear. He was propelled by an invisible force to the head of the stairs, and then—whizz! down he went in one prodigious leap, clear from the top to the first landing.

Here, in pitch-darkness, he grappled one of his assailants. For a few seconds they swayed and struggled, and then rolled down the rest of the stairs, over and over each other, grappling and clawing, each trying to tear the other's shirt off. When they rolled into the street, Carew discovered that he had hold of Charlie Gordon.

They sat up and looked at each other. Then they made a simultaneous rush for the stairs, but the street door was slammed in their faces. They kicked it violently, but without result, except that a mob of faces looked out of the first-floor window and hooted, and a bucket of water was emptied over them. A crowd collected as if by magic, and the spectacle of two gentlemen in evening dress trying to kick in the door of a shilling dancing saloon afforded it unmitigated delight.

"'Ere's two toffs got done in all right," said one.

"What O! Won't she darnce with you?" said another; and somebody from the back threw banana peel at them.

Charlie recovered his wits first. The Englishman was fairly berserk with rage, and glared round on the bystanders as if he contemplated a rush among them. The cabman put an end to the performance. He

BANJO PATERSON'S PEOPLE

was tranquil and unemotional, and he soothed them down and coaxed them into the cab. The band in the room above resumed the dreamy waltz music of "Bid me goodbye and go!" and they went.

Carew subsided into the corner, breathing hard and feeling his eye. Charlie leant forward and peered out into the darkness. They were nearly at the club before they spoke. Then he said, "Well, I'm blessed! We made a nice mess of that, didn't we?"

Jim Carew

OCTOBER 1895

Born of a thoroughbred English race,
   Well proportioned and closely knit,
Neat of figure and handsome face,
   Always ready and always fit,
Hard and wiry of limb and thew,
That was the ne'er-do-well Jim Carew.

One of the sons of the good old land—
   Many a year since his like was known;
Never a game but he took command,
   Never a sport but he held his own;
Gained at his college a triple blue—
Good as they make them was Jim Carew.

Came to grief—was it card or horse?
   Nobody asked and nobody cared;
Ship him away to the bush of course,
   Ne'er-do-well fellows are easily spared;
Only of women a tolerable few
Sorrowed at parting with Jim Carew.

Gentleman Jim on the cattle camp,
   Sitting his horse with an easy grace;
But the reckless living has left its stamp
   In the deep drawn lines of that handsome face,
And a harder look in those eyes of blue:
Prompt at a quarrel is Jim Carew.

Billy the Lasher was out for gore—
   Twelve-stone navvy with chest of hair,
When he opened out with a hungry roar
   On a ten-stone man it was hardly fair;
But his wife was wise if his face she knew
By the time you were done with him, Jim Carew.

Gentleman Jim in the stockmen's hut
   Works with them, toils with them, side by side;
As to his past—well, his lips are shut.
   "Gentleman once," say his mates with pride;
And the wildest Cornstalk can ne'er outdo
In feats of recklessness, Jim Carew.

What should he live for? A dull despair!
   Drink is his master and drags him down,
Water of Lethe that drowns all care.
   Gentleman Jim has a lot to drown,
And he reigns as king with a drunken crew,
Sinking to misery, Jim Carew.

Such is the end of the ne'er-do-well—
   Jimmy the Boozer, all down at heel;
But he straightens up when he's asked to tell
   His name and race, and a flash of steel
Still lightens up in those eyes of blue—
"I am, or—no, I *was*—Jim Carew."

GENTLEMAN JIM NO. 2

BANJO PATERSON'S PEOPLE

OUR NEW HORSE

MARCH 1890

The boys had come back from the races
   All silent and down on their luck;
They'd backed 'em, straight out and for places,
   But never a winner they struck.
They lost their good money on Slogan,
   And fell most uncommonly flat,
When Partner, the pride of the Bogan,
   Was beaten by Aristocrat.

And one said, "I move that instanter
   We sell out our horses and quit,
The brutes ought to win in a canter,
   Such trials they do when they're fit.
The last one they ran was a snorter—
   A gallop to gladden one's heart—
Two-twelve for a mile and a quarter,
   And finished as straight as a dart.

"And then when I think that they're ready
   To win me a nice little swag,
They are licked like the veriest neddy—
   They're licked from the fall of the flag.
The mare held her own to the stable,
   She died out to nothing at that,
And Partner he never seemed able
   To pace it with Aristocrat.

"And times have been bad, and the seasons
   Don't promise to be of the best;
In short, boys, there's plenty of reasons
   For giving the racing a rest.
The mare can be kept on the station—
   Her breeding is good as can be—
But Partner, his next destination
   Is rather a trouble to me.

"We can't sell him here, for they know him
   As well as the clerk of the course;
He's raced and won races till, blow him,
   He's done as a handicap horse.
A jady, uncertain performer,
   They weight him right out of the hunt,
And clap it on warmer and warmer
   Whenever he gets near the front.

"It's no use to paint him or to dot him
   Or put any 'fake' on his brand,
For bushmen are smart, and they'd spot him
   In any saleyard in the land.
The folk about here could all tell him,
   Could swear to each separate hair;
Let us send him to Sydney and sell him,
   There's plenty of Jugginses there.

"We'll call him a maiden, and treat 'em
   To trials will open their eyes,
We'll run their best horses and beat 'em,
   And then won't they think him a prize.
I pity the fellow that buys him,
   He'll find in a very short space,
No matter how highly he tries him,
   The beggar won't *race* in a race."

Next week, under "Seller and Buyer",
   Appeared in the *Daily Gazette*:
"A racehorse for sale, and a flyer;
   Has never been started as yet;
A trial will show what his pace is;
   The buyer can get him in light,
And win all the handicap races.
   Apply here before Wednesday night."

He sold for a hundred and thirty,
   Because of a gallop he had
One morning with Bluefish and Bertie,
   And donkey-licked both of 'em bad.
And when the old horse had departed,
   The life on the station grew tame;
The racetrack was dull and deserted,
   The boys had gone back on the game.

The winter rolled by, and the station
   Was green with the garland of spring,
A spirit of glad exultation
   Awoke in each animate thing.
And all the old love, the old longing,
   Broke out in the breasts of the boys,
The visions of racing came thronging
   With all its delirious joys.

The rushing of floods in their courses,
   The rattle of rain on the roofs
Recalled the fierce rush of the horses,
   The thunder of galloping hoofs.
And soon one broke out: "I can suffer
   No longer the life of a slug,
The man that don't race is a duffer,
   Let's have one more run for the mug.

"Why, *everything* races, no matter
   Whatever its method may be:
The waterfowl hold a regatta;
   The possums run heats up a tree;
The emus are constantly sprinting
   A handicap out on the plain;
It seems like all nature was hinting,
   'Tis time to be at it again.

THE STATION HANDS' QUARTERS

BANJO PATERSON'S PEOPLE

"The cockatoo parrots are talking
  Of races to faraway lands;
The native companions are walking
  As go-as-you-please on the sands;
The little foals gallop for pastime;
  The wallabies race down the gap;
Let's try it once more for the last time,
  Bring out the old jacket and cap.

"And now for a horse; we might try one
  Of those that are bred on the place,
But I think it better to buy one,
  A horse that has proved he can race.
Let us send down to Sydney to Skinner,
  A thorough good judge who can ride,
And ask him to buy us a spinner
  To clean out the whole countryside."

They wrote him a letter as follows:
  "We want you to buy us a horse;
He must have the speed to catch swallows,
  And stamina with it of course.
The price ain't a thing that'll grieve us,
  It's getting a bad 'un annoys
The undersigned blokes, and believe us,
  We're yours to a cinder, 'The boys'."

He answered: "I've bought you a hummer,
  A horse that has never been raced;
I saw him run over the Drummer,
  He held him outclassed and outpaced.
His breeding's not known, but they state he
  Is born of a thoroughbred strain,
I paid them a hundred and eighty,
  And started the horse in the train."

They met him—alas, that these verses
  Aren't up to the subject's demands—
Can't set forth their eloquent curses,
  For Partner was back on their hands.
They went in to meet him in gladness,
  They opened his box with delight—
A silent procession of sadness
  They crept to the station at night.

And life has grown dull on the station,
  The boys are all silent and slow;
Their work is a daily vexation,
  And sport is unknown to them now.
Whenever they think how they stranded,
  They squeal just like guinea-pigs squeal;
They bit their own hook, and were landed
  With fifty pounds' loss on the deal.

SPRINGTIME ON THE STATION

An Idyll of Dandaloo

DECEMBER 1889

On western plains, where shade is not,
   'Neath summer skies of cloudless blue,
Where all is dry and all is hot,
   There stands the town of Dandaloo—
A township where life's total sum
Is sleep, diversified with rum.

Its grass-grown streets with dust are deep,
   'Twere vain endeavour to express
The dreamless silence of its sleep,
   Its wide, expansive drunkenness.
The yearly races mostly drew
A lively crowd to Dandaloo.

There came a sportsman from the east,
   The eastern land where sportsmen blow,
And brought with him a speedy beast—
   A speedy beast as horses go.
He came afar in hope to "do"
The little town of Dandaloo.

Now this was weak of him, I wot—
   Exceeding weak, it seemed to me—
For we in Dandaloo were not
   The Jugginses we seemed to be;
In fact, we rather thought we knew
Our book by heart in Dandaloo.

We held a meeting at the bar,
   And met the question fair and square—
"We've stumped the country near and far
   To raise the cash for races here;
We've got a hundred pounds or two—
Not half so bad for Dandaloo.

"And now, it seems, we have to be
   Cleaned out by this here Sydney bloke,
With his imported horse; and he
   Will scoop the pool and leave us broke.
Shall we sit still, and make no fuss
While this chap climbs all over us?"

The races came to Dandaloo,
   And all the cornstalks from the west,
On ev'ry kind of moke and screw,
   Came forth in all their glory drest.
The stranger's horse, as hard as nails,
Look'd fit to run for New South Wales.

He won the race by half a length—
   Quite half a length, it seemed to me—
But Dandaloo, with all its strength,
   Roared out, "Dead heat!" most fervently;
And, after hesitation meet,
The judge's verdict was "Dead heat!"

And many men there were could tell
   What gave the verdict extra force:
The stewards, and the judge as well—
   They all had backed the second horse.
For things like this they sometimes do
In larger towns than Dandaloo.

They ran it off; the stranger won,
   Hands down, by near a hundred yards.
He smiled to think his troubles done;
   But Dandaloo held all the cards.
They went to scale and—cruel fate!—
His jockey turned out underweight.

Perhaps they'd tampered with the scale!
   I cannot tell. I only know
It weighed him *out* all right. I fail
   To paint that Sydney sportsman's woe.
He said the stewards were a crew
Of low-lived thieves in Dandaloo.

He lifted up his voice, irate,
   And swore till all the air was blue;
So then we rose to vindicate
   The dignity of Dandaloo.
"Look here," said we, "you must not poke
Such oaths at us poor country folk."

We rode him softly on a rail,
   We shied at him, in careless glee,
Some large tomatoes, rank and stale,
   And eggs of great antiquity—
Their wild, unholy fragrance flew
About the town of Dandaloo.

He left the town at break of day,
   He led his racehorse through the streets,
And now he tells the tale, they say,
   To every racing man he meets.
And Sydney sportsmen all eschew
The atmosphere of Dandaloo.

BANJO PATERSON'S PEOPLE

DANDALOO

TAR AND FEATHERS
SEPTEMBER 1889

Oh, the circus swooped down
  On the Narrabri town,
For the Narrabri populace moneyed are;
  And the circus man smiled
  At the folk he beguiled
To come all the distance from Gunnedah.

But a juvenile smart,
  Who objected to "part",
Went in "on the nod", and to do it he
  Crawled in through a crack
  In the tent at the back,
For the boy had no slight ingenuity.

Says he, with a grin,
  "*That's* the way to get in,
But I reckon I'd better be quiet, or
  They'll spiflicate me" –
  And he chuckled, for he
Had the loan of the circus proprietor.

But the showman astute
  On that wily galoot,
Soon dropped, and you'll say that he leathered him.
  Not he! With a grim
  Sort of humorous whim
He took him and tarred him and feathered him.

Says he, "You can go
  As a star with Jo-Jo,
And knock ev'ry Injun and Arab wry,
  With your name and your trade
  On the posters displayed,
'The Feathered What Is It from Narrabri!'"

Next day for his freak
  By a Narrabri beak
He was jawed with a deal of verbosity.
  For his only appeal
  Was "professional zeal" –
"He wanted another monstrosity."

Said his worship, "Begob!
  You are fined for-r-r-ty bob!
An' six shillin's costs to the *clurk*," he says;
  Yet the Narrabri Joy,
  Half-bird and half-boy,
Has a "down" on himself and on circuses.

THE SHOWMAN

BANJO PATERSON'S PEOPLE

SALTBUSH BILL

DECEMBER 1894

Now this is the law of the Overland that all in the west obey,
A man must cover with travelling sheep a six-mile stage a day;
But this is the law which the drovers make, right easily understood,
They travel their stage where the grass is bad, but they camp where the grass is good;
They camp, and they ravage the squatter's grass till never a blade remains,
Then they drift away as the white clouds drift on the edge of the saltbush plains,
From camp to camp and from run to run they battle it hand to hand,
For a blade of grass and the right to pass on the track of the Overland.

For this is the law of the Great Stock Routes, 'tis written in white and black—
The man that goes with a travelling mob must keep to a half-mile track;
And the drovers keep to a half-mile track on the runs where the grass is dead,
But they spread their sheep in a well-grassed run till they go with a two-mile spread.
So the squatters hurry the drovers on from dawn till the fall of night,
And the squatters' dogs and the drovers' dogs get mixed in a deadly fight;
Yet the squatters' men, though they hunt the mob, are willing the peace to keep,
For the drovers learn how to use their hands when they go with the travelling sheep;
But this is the tale of a Jackaroo that came from a foreign strand,
And the fight that he fought with Saltbush Bill, the King of the Overland.

Now Saltbush Bill was a drover tough, as ever the country knew,
He had fought his way on the Great Stock Routes from the sea to the Big Barcoo;
He could tell when he came to a friendly run that gave him a chance to spread,
And he knew where the hungry owners were that hurried his sheep ahead;
He was drifting down in the Eighty drought with a mob that could scarcely creep,
(When the kangaroos by the thousands starve, it is rough on the travelling sheep.)
And he camped one night at the crossing place on the edge of the Wilga run,
"We must manage a feed for them here," he said, "or the half of the mob are done!"
So he spread them out when they left the camp wherever they liked to go,
Till he grew aware of a Jackaroo with a station hand in tow,
And they set to work on the straggling sheep, and with many a stockwhip crack
They forced them in where the grass was dead in the space of the half-mile track;
So William prayed that the hand of fate might suddenly strike him blue
But he'd get some grass for his starving sheep in the teeth of that Jackaroo.
So he turned and he cursed the Jackaroo, he cursed him alive or dead,
From the soles of his great unwieldy feet to the crown of his ugly head,
With an extra curse on the moke he rode and the cur at his heels that ran,
Till the Jackaroo from his horse got down and he went for the drover man;
With the station hand for his picker-up, though the sheep ran loose the while,
They battled it out on the saltbush plain in the regular prize ring style.

Now, the new chum fought for his honour's sake and the pride of the English race,
But the drover fought for his daily bread with a smile on his bearded face;
So he shifted ground and he sparred for wind and he made it a lengthy mill,
And from time to time as his scouts came in they whispered to Saltbush Bill—
"We have spread the sheep with a two-mile spread, and the grass it is something grand,
You must stick to him, Bill, for another round for the pride of the Overland."

The new chum made it a rushing fight, though never a blow got home,
Till the sun rode high in the cloudless sky and glared at the brick-red loam,
Till the sheep drew in to the shelter trees and settled them down to rest,
Then the driver said he would fight no more and he gave his opponent best.
So the new chum rode to the homestead straight and he told them a story grand

SALTBUSH BILL

BANJO PATERSON'S PEOPLE

Of the desperate fight that he fought that day with the King of the Overland.
And the tale went home to the public schools of the pluck of the English swell,
How the drover fought for his very life, but blood in the end must tell.
But the travelling sheep and the Wilga sheep were boxed on the Old Man Plain.
'Twas a full week's work ere they drafted out and hunted them off again,
With a week's good grass in their wretched hides, with a curse and a stockwhip crack,
They hunted them off on the road once more to starve on the half-mile track.
And Saltbush Bill, on the Overland, will many a time recite
How the best day's work that ever he did was the day that he lost the fight.

SALTBUSH BILL'S INQUEST

BANJO PATERSON'S PEOPLE

A Bushman's Song

DECEMBER 1892

I'm travellin' down the Castlereagh, and I'm a station hand,
I'm handy with the ropin' pole, I'm handy with the brand,
And I can ride a rowdy colt, or swing the axe all day,
But there's no demand for a station hand along the Castlereagh.

So it's shift, boys, shift, for there isn't the slightest doubt
That we've got to make a shift to the stations further out
With the packhorse runnin' after, for he follows like a dog,
We must strike across the country at the old jig-jog.

This old black horse I'm riding—if you'll notice what's his brand,
He wears the crooked R, you see—none better in the land.
He takes a lot of beatin', and the other day we tried,
For a bit of a joke, with a racing bloke, for twenty pounds aside.

It was shift, boys, shift, for there wasn't the slightest doubt,
That I had to make him shift, for the money was nearly out;
But he cantered home a winner, with the other one at the flog—
He's a red-hot sort to pick up with his old jig-jog.

I asked a cove for shearin' once along the Marthaguy:
"We shear non-union, here," says he. "I call it scab," says I.
I looked along the shearin' floor before I turned to go—
There were eight or ten dashed Chinamen a-shearin' in a row.

It was shift, boys, shift, for there wasn't the slightest doubt
It was time to make a shift with the leprosy about.
So I saddled up my horses, and I whistled to my dog,
And I left his scabby station at the old jig-jog.

I went to Illawarra where my brother's got a farm,
He has to ask his landlord's leave before he lifts his arm;
The landlord owns the countryside—man, woman, dog and cat,
They haven't the cheek to dare to speak without they touch their hat.

It was shift, boys, shift, for there wasn't the slightest doubt
Their little landlord god and I would soon have fallen out;
Was I to touch my hat to him?—was I his bloomin' dog?
So I makes for up the country at the old jig-jog.

But it's time that I was movin', I've a mighty way to go
Till I drink artesian water from a thousand feet below;
Till I meet the overlanders with the cattle comin' down,
And I'll work a while till I make a pile, then have a spree in town.

So, it's shift, boys, shift, for there isn't the slightest doubt
We've got to make a shift to the stations further out;
The packhorse runs behind us, for he follows like a dog,
And we cross a lot of country at the old jig-jog.

THE JOBLESS JACKAROO

BANJO PATERSON'S PEOPLE

The City of Dreadful Thirst

DECEMBER 1899

The stranger came from Narromine and made his little joke—
"They say we folks in Narromine are narrow-minded folk.
But all the smartest men down here are puzzled to define
A kind of new phenomenon that came to Narromine.

"Last summer up in Narromine 'twas gettin' rather warm—
Two hundred in the water bag and lookin' like a storm—
We all were in the private bar, the coolest place in town,
When out across the stretch of plain a cloud came rollin' down.

"We don't respect the clouds up there, they fill us with disgust,
They mostly bring a Bogan shower—three raindrops and some dust;
But each man, simultaneous-like, to each man said, 'I think
That cloud suggests it's up to us to have another drink!'

"There's clouds of rain and clouds of dust—we've heard of them before,
And sometimes in the daily press we read of 'clouds of war':
But—if this ain't the Gospel truth I hope that I may burst—
That cloud that came to Narromine was just a cloud of thirst.

"It wasn't like a common cloud, 'twas more a sort of haze;
It settled down about the streets, and stopped for days and days,
And not a drop of dew could fall and not a sunbeam shine
To pierce that dismal sort of mist that hung on Narromine.

"Oh, Lord! we had a dreadful time beneath that cloud of thirst!
We all chucked-up our daily work and went upon the burst.
The very blacks about the town that used to cadge for grub,
They made an organised attack and tried to loot the pub.

"We couldn't leave the private bar no matter how we tried;
Shearers and squatters, union men and blacklegs side by side
Were drinkin' there and dursn't move, for each was sure, he said,
Before he'd get a half a mile the thirst would strike him dead!

"We drank until the drink gave out, we searched from room to room,
And round the pub, like drunken ghosts, went howling through the gloom.
The shearers found some kerosene and settled down again,
But all the squatter chaps and I, we staggered to the train.

"And, once outside the cloud of thirst, we felt as right as pie,
But while we stopped about the town we had to drink or die.
But now I hear it's safe enough, I'm going back to work
Because they say the cloud of thirst has shifted on to Bourke.

"But when you see those clouds about—like this one over here—
All white and frothy at the top, just like a pint of beer,
It's time to go and have a drink, for if that cloud should burst
You'd find the drink would all be gone, for that's a cloud of thirst!"

We stood the man from Narromine a pint of half-and-half;
He drank it off without a gasp in one tremendous quaff;
"I joined some friends last night," he said, "in what *they* called a spree;
But after Narromine 'twas just a holiday to me."

And now beyond the western range, where sunset skies are red,
And clouds of dust, and clouds of thirst, go drifting overhead,
The railway train is taking back, along the western line,
That narrow-minded person on his road to Narromine.

BANJO PATERSON'S PEOPLE

IN THE EULO QUEEN'S PUB

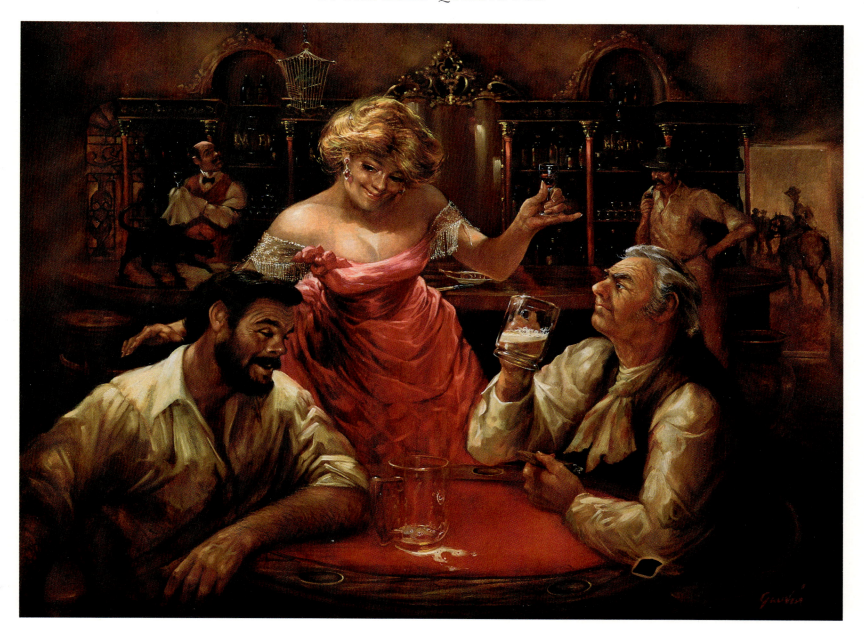

BANJO PATERSON'S PEOPLE

T.Y.S.O.N.

DECEMBER 1898

Across the Queensland border line
   The mobs of cattle go;
They travel down in sun and shine
   On dusty stage, and slow.
The drovers, riding slowly on
   To let the cattle spread,
Will say, "Here's one old landmark gone,
   For old man Tyson's dead."

What tales there'll be in every camp
   By men that Tyson knew;
The swagmen, meeting on the tramp,
   Will yarn the long day through,
And tell of how he passed as "Brown",
   And fooled the local men.
"But not for me—I struck the town,
And passed the message further down;
   That's T.Y.S.O.N.!"

There stands a little country town
   Beyond the border line,
Where dusty roads go up and down,
   And banks with pubs combine.
A stranger came to cash a cheque,
   Few were the words he said;
A handkerchief about his neck,
   An old hat on his head.

A long, grey stranger, eagle-eyed,
   "You know me? Of course you do."
"It's not my work," the boss replied,
   "To know such tramps as you."
"Well, look here, Mister, don't be flash,"
   Replied the stranger then,
"I never care to make a splash,
I'm simple—but I've got the cash,
   I'm T.Y.S.O.N."

But in that last great drafting yard,
   Where Peter keeps the gate,
And souls of sinners find it barred,
   And go to meet their fate;
There's one who ought to enter in,
   For good deeds done on earth;
Such deeds as merit ought to win,
   Kind deeds of sterling worth.

Not by the straight and narrow gate,
   Reserved for wealthy men,
But through the big gate, opened wide,
The grizzled figure, eagle-eyed,
   Will travel through—and then
Old Peter'll say, "We pass him through,
There's many a thing he used to do,
Good-hearted things that no one knew;
   That's T.Y.S.O.N."

BANJO PATERSON'S PEOPLE

COUNTRY TOWN

BANJO PATERSON'S PEOPLE

A Dream of the Melbourne Cup

A LONG WAY AFTER GORDON   OCTOBER 1886

Bring me a quart of colonial beer
And some doughy damper to make good cheer,
   I must make a heavy dinner;
Heavily dine and heavily sup
Of indigestible things full-up,
Next month they run the Melbourne Cup,
   And I have to dream the winner.

Stoke it in, boys! the half-cooked ham,
The rich ragout and the charming cham,
   I've got to mix my liquor;
Give me a gander's gaunt hind leg,
Hard and tough as a wooden peg,
And I'll grease it down with a hard-boiled egg,
   'Twill make me dream the quicker.

Now I am full of fearful feed,
Now I may dream a race indeed,
   In my restless troubled slumber;
While the nightmares race through my heated brain
And their devil riders spur amain,
The tip for the Cup will reward my pain,
   And I'll spot the winning number.

Thousands and thousands and thousands more,
Like sands on the white Pacific shore,
   The crowding people cluster;
For evermore it's the story old,
While races are bought and backers are sold,
Drawn by the greed of the gain of gold,
   In their thousands still they muster.

And the bookies' cries grow fierce and hot,
"I'll lay the Cup! The double, if not!"
   "Five monkeys, Little John, sir!"
"Here's fives bar one, I lay, I lay!"

And so they shout through the live-long day,
And stick to the game that is sure to pay,
   While fools put money on, sir!

And now in my dream I seem to go
And bet with a "book" that I seem to know—
   A Hebrew moneylender;
A million to five is the price I get—
Not bad! but before I book the bet
The horse's name I clean forget,
   His number and even gender.

Now for the start, and here they come,
And the hoof-strokes roar like a mighty drum
   Beat by a hand unsteady;
They come like a rushing, roaring flood,
Hurrah for the speed of the Chester blood!
For Acme is making the pace so good
   There are some of 'em done already.

But round the back she begins to tire,
And a mighty shout goes up: "Crossfire!"
   The magpie jacket's leading;
And Crossfire challenges fierce and bold,
And the lead she'll have and the lead she'll hold,
But at length gives way to the black and gold,
   Which away to the front is speeding.

Carry them on and keep it up—
A flying race is the Melbourne Cup,
   You must race and stay to win it;
And old Commotion, Victoria's pride,
Now takes the lead with his raking stride,
And a might roar goes far and wide—
   "There's only Commotion in it!"

But one draws out from the beaten ruck,
And up on the rails by a piece of luck
   He comes in a style that's clever;
"It's Trident! Trident! Hurrah for Hales!
Go at 'em now while their courage fails;"
"Trident! Trident! for New South Wales!"
   "The blue and white for ever!"

Under the whip! With the ears flat back,
Under the whip! Though the sinews crack,
   No sign of the base white feather;
Stick to it now for your breeding's sake,
Stick to it now though your hearts should break,
While the yells and roars make
   the grandstand shake,
   They come down the straight together.

Trident slowly forges ahead,
The fierce whips cut and the spurs are red,
   The pace is undiminished;
Now for the Panics that never fail!
But many a backer's face grows pale
As old Commotion swings his tail
   And swerves—and the Cup is finished.

And now in my dream it all comes back:
I bet my coin on the Sydney crack,
   A million I've won, no question!
Give me my money, you hook-nosed hog!
Give me my money, bookmaking dog!
But he disappears in a kind of fog,
   And I wake with "the indigestion".

BANJO PATERSON'S PEOPLE

MELBOURNE CUP BOOKIES

BANJO PATERSON'S PEOPLE

Pioneers

DECEMBER 1896

They came of bold and roving stock that would not fixed abide;
They were the sons of field and flock since e'er they learned to ride;
We may not hope to see such men in these degenerate years
As those explorers of the bush—the brave old pioneers.

'Twas they who rode the trackless bush in heat and storm and drought;
'Twas they that heard the master-word that called them further out;
'Twas they that followed up the trail the mountain cattle made
And pressed across the mighty range where now their bones are laid.

But now the times are dull and slow, the brave old days are dead
When hardy bushmen started out, and forced their way ahead
By tangled scrub and forests grim towards the unknown west,
And spied the far-off promised land from off the ranges' crest.

Oh! ye, that sleep in lonely graves by far-off ridge and plain,
We drink to you in silence now as Christmas comes again,
The men who fought the wilderness through rough, unsettled years—
The founders of our nation's life, the brave old pioneers.

GOING BUSH AGAIN

BANJO PATERSON'S PEOPLE

THE RIDERS IN THE STAND

AUGUST 1903

There's some that ride the Robbo style, and bump at every stride;
While others sit a long way back, to get a longer ride.
There's some that ride like sailors do, with legs, and arms, and teeth;
And some ride on the horse's neck, and some ride underneath.

But all the finest horsemen out—the men to beat the band—
You'll find amongst the crowd that ride their races in the stand.
They'll say, "He had the race in hand, and lost it in the straight".
They'll show how Godby came too soon, and Barden came too late.

They'll say Chevalley lost his nerve, and Regan lost his head;
They'll tell how one was "livened up" and something else was "dead"—
In fact, the race was never run on sea, or sky, or land,
But what you'd get it better done by riders in the stand.

The rule holds good in everything in life's uncertain fight:
You'll find the winner can't go wrong, the loser can't go right.
You ride a slashing race, and lose—by one and all you're banned!
Ride like a bag of flour, and win—they'll cheer you in the stand.

THE LAST RACE

In the Droving Days

JUNE 1891

"Only a pound," said the auctioneer,
"Only a pound; and I'm standing here
Selling this animal, gain or loss.
Only a pound for the drover's horse;
One of the sort that was ne'er afraid,
One of the boys of the Old Brigade;
Thoroughly honest and game, I'll swear,
Only a little the worse for wear;
Plenty as bad to be seen in town,
Give me a bid and I'll knock him down;
Sold as he stands, and without recourse,
Give me a bid for the drover's horse."

Loitering there in an aimless way
Somehow I noticed the poor old grey,
Weary and battered and screwed, of course,
Yet when I noticed the old grey horse,
The rough bush saddle, and single rein
Of the bridle laid on his tangled mane,
Straightway the crowd and the auctioneer
Seemed on a sudden to disappear,
Melted away in a kind of haze,
For my heart went back to the droving days.

Back to the road, and I crossed again
Over the miles of the saltbush plain—
The shining plain that is said to be
The dried-up bed of an inland sea,
Where the air so dry and so clear and bright
Refracts the sun with a wondrous light,
And out in the dim horizon makes
The deep blue gleam of the phantom lakes.

At dawn of day we would feel the breeze
That stirred the boughs of the sleeping trees,
And brought a breath of the fragrance rare
That comes and goes in that scented air;
For the trees and grass and the shrubs contain
A dry sweet scent on the saltbush plain.
For those that love it and understand,
The saltbush plain is a wonderland.
A wondrous country, where nature's ways
Were revealed to me in the droving days.

We saw the fleet wild horses pass,
And the kangaroos through the Mitchell grass,
The emu ran with her frightened brood
All unmolested and unpursued.
But there rose a shout and a wild hubbub
When the dingo raced for his native scrub,
And he paid right dear for his stolen meals
With the drovers' dogs at his wretched heels.
For we ran him down at a rattling pace,
While the pack horse joined in the stirring chase.
And a wild halloo at the kill we'd raise—
We were light of heart in the droving days.

'Twas a drover's horse, and my hand again
Made a move to close on a fancied rein.
For I felt the swing and the easy stride
Of the grand old horse that I used to ride
In drought or plenty, in good or ill,
That same old steed was my comrade still;
The old grey horse with his honest ways
Was a mate to me in the droving days.

When we kept our watch in the cold and damp,
If the cattle broke from the sleeping camp,
Over the flats and across the plain,
With my head bent down on his waving mane,
Through the boughs above and the stumps below
On the darkest night I would let him go
At a racing speed; he would choose his course,
And my life was safe with the old grey horse.
But man and horse had a favourite job,
When an outlaw broke from a station mob,
With a right good will was the stockwhip plied,
As the old horse raced at the straggler's side,
And the greenhide whip such a weal would raise,
We could use the whip in the droving days.

"Only a pound!" and this was the end—
Only a pound for the drover's friend.
The drover's friend that had seen his day,
And now was worthless, and cast away
With a broken knee and a broken heart
To be flogged and starved in a hawker's cart.
Well, I made a bid for a sense of shame
And the memories dear of the good old game.

"Thank you? Guinea! and cheap at that!
Against you there in the curly hat!
Only a guinea, and one more chance,
Down he goes if there's no advance,
Third, and the last time, one! two! three!"
And the old grey horse was knocked down to me.
And now he's wandering, fat and sleek,
On the lucerne flats by the Homestead Creek;
I dare not ride him for fear he'd fall,
But he does a journey to beat them all,
For though he scarcely a trot can raise,
He can take me back to the droving days.

BANJO PATERSON'S PEOPLE

AT AUCTION

BANJO PATERSON'S PEOPLE

WHEN DACEY RODE THE MULE

JULY 1893

'Twas in a small, up-country town,
   When we were boys at school,
There came a circus with a clown
   And with a bucking mule.
The clown announced a scheme they had—
   The mule was such a king—
They'd give a crown to any lad
   Who'd ride him round the ring.
And, gentle reader, do not scoff
   Nor think the man a fool,
To buck a porous plaster off
   Was pastime to that mule.

The boys got on—he bucked like sin—
   He threw them in the dirt,
And then the clown would raise a grin
   By asking, "Were they hurt?"
But Johnny Dacey came one night,
   The crack of all the school,
Said he, "I'll win the crown all right,
   Bring in your bucking mule."
The elephant went off his trunk,
   The monkey played the fool
And all the band got blazing drunk
   When Dacey rode the mule.

But soon there rose an awful shout
   Of laughter, when the clown,
From somewhere in his pants drew out
   A little paper crown.
He placed the crown on Dacey's head,
   While Dacey looked a fool,

"Now, there's your crown, my lad," he said,
   "For riding of the mule!"
The band struck up with "Killaloe",
   And "Rule Britannia, Rule",
And "Young Man from the Country", too,
   When Dacey rode the mule.

Then Dacey, in a furious rage,
   For vengeance on the show
Ascended to the monkey's cage
   And let the monkeys go;
The blue-tailed ape and chimpanzee
   He turned abroad to roam;
Good faith! It was a sight to see
   The people step for home.
For big baboons with canine snout
   Are spiteful, as a rule,
The people didn't sit it out
   When Dacey rode the mule.

And from the beasts that did escape
   The bushmen all declare
Were born some creatures partly ape
   And partly native bear.
They're rather few and far between;
   The race is nearly spent;
But some of them may still be seen
   In Sydney Parliament.
And when those legislators fight,
   And drink, and act the fool—
It all commenced that wretched night
   When Dacey rode the mule.

BANJO PATERSON'S PEOPLE

DACEY AND THE MULE

WITH THE CATTLE

SEPTEMBER 1896

The drought is down on field and flock,
   The river bed is dry;
And we shift the starving stock
   Before the cattle die.
We muster up with weary hearts
   At breaking of the day,
And turn our heads to foreign parts,
   To take the stock away.
      And it's hunt 'em up and dog 'em,
      And it's get the whip and flog 'em,
For it's weary work is droving when they're dying every day;
      By stock routes bare and eaten,
      On dusty roads and beaten,
With half a chance to save their lives we take the stock away.

We cannot use the whip for shame
   On beasts that crawl along;
We have to drop the weak and lame,
   And try to save the strong;
The wrath of God is on the track,
   The drought fiend holds his sway,
With blows and cries and stockwhip crack
   We take the stock away.
      As they fall we leave them lying,
      With the crows to watch them dying,
Grim sextons of the Overland that fasten on their prey;
      By the fiery dust storm drifting,
      And the mocking mirage shifting,
In heat and drought and hopeless pain we take the stock away.

In dull despair the days go by
   With never hope of change,
But every stage we draw more nigh
   Towards the mountain range;
And some may live to climb the pass,
   And reach the great plateau,
And revel in the mountain grass,
   By streamlets fed with snow.
      As the mountain wind is blowing
      It starts the cattle lowing,
And calling to each other down the dusty long array;
      And there speaks a grizzled drover:
      "Well, thank God, the worst is over,
The creatures smell the mountain grass that's twenty miles away."

They press towards the mountain grass,
   They look with eager eyes
Along the rugged stony pass,
   That slopes towards the skies;
Their feet may bleed from rocks and stones,
   But though the blood-drop starts,
They struggle on with stifled groans,
   For hope is in their hearts.
      And the cattle that are leading,
      Though their feet are worn and bleeding,
Are breaking to a kind of run—pull up, and let them go!
      For the mountain wind is blowing,
      And the mountain grass is growing,
They settle down by running streams ice-cold with melted snow.

The days are done of heat and drought
   Upon the stricken plain;
The wind has shifted right about,
   And brought the welcome rain;
The river runs with sullen roar,
   All flecked with yellow foam,
And we must take the road once more,
   To bring the cattle home.
      And it's "Lads! we'll raise a chorus,
      There's a pleasant trip before us."
And the horses bound beneath us as we start them down the track;
      And the drovers canter, singing,

BANJO PATERSON'S PEOPLE

THE STOCKMEN

BANJO PATERSON'S PEOPLE

Through the sweet green grasses springing,
Towards the far-off mountain land, to bring the cattle back.

Are these the beasts we brought away
  That move so lively now?
They scatter off like flying spray
  Across the mountain's brow;
And dashing down the rugged range
  We hear the stockwhip crack,
Good faith, it is a welcome change
  To bring such cattle back.
    And it's "Steady down the lead there!"
    And it's "Let 'em stop and feed there!"
For they're wild as mountain eagles and their sides are all afoam;
    But they're settling down already,
    And they'll travel nice and steady,
With cheery call and jest and song we fetch the cattle home.

We have to watch them close at night
  For fear they'll make a rush,
And break away in headlong flight
  Across the open bush;
And by the campfire's cheery blaze,
  With mellow voice and strong,

We hear the lonely watchman raise
  The Overlander's song:
    "Oh! it's when we're done with roving,
    With the camping and the droving,
It's homeward down the Bland we'll go, and never more we'll roam;"
    While the stars shine out above us,
    Like the eyes of those who love us—
The eyes of those who watch and wait to greet the cattle home.

The plains are all awave with grass,
  The skies are deepest blue;
And leisurely the cattle pass
  And feed the long day through;
But when we sight the station gate,
  We make the stockwhips crack,
A welcome sound to those who wait
  To greet the cattle back:
    And through the twilight falling
    We hear their voices calling,
As the cattle splash across the ford and churn it into foam;
    And the children run to meet us,
    And our wives and sweethearts greet us,
Their heroes from the Overland who brought the cattle home.

THE OVERLANDERS

BANJO PATERSON'S PEOPLE

THE WILD CATTLE

from *AN OUTBACK MARRIAGE*

THEY RODE OUT, day after day, through interminable stretches of dull timbered country, or over blazing plains waving with long grass. Here they came on mobs of half-wild cattle, all bearing the same brand, a huge RL5. These were not mustered into a yard or counted, except roughly. Gordon was not completing a purchase, but simply taking over what were there—many or few, good or bad, he could only take what he found.

Miles and miles they rode, always in the blazing heat, camping for a couple of hours in the middle of the day. To the Englishman it seemed always the merest chance that they found the cattle, and accident that they got home again. At rare intervals they came upon substantial mustering-yards, where the calves were brought for branding; near these a rough hut had been constructed, so that they could camp there at night, instead of returning to the head station.

They always slept out of doors. In the intense heat it was no hardship, and the huts, as a rule, fairly jumped with fleas. Once they camped alongside a big lagoon, on whose surface were huge pink and blue water-lilies and rushes, and vast flocks of wild fowl. After the stretches of blazing plain and dull timber this glimpse of water was inexpressibly refreshing.

On their way back they struck new country, great stretches of almost impenetrable scrub, tropical jungle, and belts of bamboo. In this cover wild cattle evidently abounded, for they frequently heard the bellow of the bulls.

"There should be a terrible lot of wild cattle here," said Charlie. "Don't you ever get any out of the scrubs?"

"Oh, yes, we moonlight for 'em," said Considine. "We take coachers out. We have a very fair coaching mob. Some of our coachers are as quick as racehorses, and they'll hustle wild cattle away from the scrub just as if they understood."

"What do you mean by coachers?" asked Carew. "Not cattle that go in carts, eh?"

"Carts, no. The way we get wild cattle hereabouts is to take out a mob of quiet cattle, what we call coachers, and let 'em feed in the moonlight alongside the scrub, while we wait back out o' the road and watch 'em. When the wild cattle come out, they run over to see the coachers and we dash up and cut 'em off from the scrub, and hustle 'em together into the open. It's good sport, Mister. We might try a dash at it, if you like, before we go back; it's moonlight now."

"Let's have a try tonight," said Gordon. "Are your coachers handy?"

"Yairs. They feed near the house. I'll send 'em on with the gins tonight."

When they got back that evening, Carew was so dead-tired that he wished the wild cattle expedition at Jericho. But Considine and Charlie were in great form, directing, arguing, and planning the expedition. One of the black boys rode out, and returned driving a big mob of horses that dashed into the yard at full gallop. The gins and the black boys caught fresh mounts out of these and started away, driving some fifty head of cattle selected from a mob that made their headquarters within a few miles of the house. Most of them were old stagers, and strung away in the evening quite tranquilly, while the blacks, always

BANJO PATERSON'S PEOPLE

TURNING THE WILD CATTLE

smoking, rode listlessly after. Considine produced two stockwhips, and gave one to Charlie.

"No good givin' you one, Mister," he said to Carew. "You'd hang yourself with it most likely. I've got a rare good horse for you—old Smoked Beef. He'd moonlight cattle by himself, I believe. You'd better have a pistol, though."

"What for?" asked Carew, as Considine produced three very heavy navy revolvers and a bag of cartridges.

"To shoot any beast that won't stay with the mob. Some of 'em won't be stopped. They have to go. Well, if one goes, the rest keep trying to follow, and no forty men will hold 'em back. You just keep your eyes open, and if a beast breaks out in spite of the whips, you shoot him if the blacks tell you. See?"

"Where am I to shoot him?"

"Shoot him any place. In the earhole, or the shoulder, or the ribs, or the flank. Any place at all. Shoot him all over if you like. One or two bullets don't hurt a beast. It takes a leadmine to kill some of 'em."

"Do the blacks shoot?" asked Charlie.

"No, I don't never trust no blacks with firearms. One boy knifes well, though. Races alongside and knifes 'em."

This seemed a fairly difficult performance; while the Englishman was wondering how it would be carried out, they made a start. They rode mile after mile in the yellow moonlight, until they discerned a mob of cattle feeding placidly near some scrub. They whistled to the blacks, and all rode away down wind to a spot on the edge of the plain, a considerable distance from the cattle.

Here they dismounted and waited, Considine and Charlie talking occasionally in low tones, while the blacks sat silent, holding their horses. Carew lay down on the long dry grass and gazed away over the plain. His horse stood over him with head down, apparently sleeping. Far away under the moon, in vague patches of light and shade, the cattle were feeding. Hours seemed to pass, and Carew almost fell asleep.

Suddenly a long-drawn bellow, the angry challenge of a bull, broke the silence. A mob of wild cattle were evidently coming along the edge of the scrub, and had caught scent of the strangers. Again the bull roared; there is no animal on earth with so emphatically warlike a note as the wild bull when advancing to meet a strange mob. The quiet cattle answered with plaintive, long-drawn lowings, and the din became general as the two lots met.

"Let 'em get well mixed up," said Considine quietly, tightening his girths, and swinging into the saddle. Everyone followed his example. Carew was shaking with excitement. Angry bellowing now arose from the cattle, which were apparently horning one another—such being their manner of greeting.

Considine said, "There's a big lot there. Hope to blazes we can hold 'em. Are you ready, Mister?"

"Yes, I'm ready," replied Carew.

"Come on, then. We'll sneak up slowly at first, but once I start galloping let your horse go as fast as he likes, and trust him altogether. Don't pull him at all, or he'll break your neck."

They started slowly in Indian file, keeping well in the shadow of the scrub. The horses picked their way through the outlying saplings and bushes, until suddenly Considine bent forward on his horse's neck, and said, "Come on!"

What a ride that was! The inexperienced reader is apt to imagine that because a plain is level, it is smooth, but no greater fallacy exists. The surface of a plain is always bad galloping. The rain washes away the soil from between the tussocks, which stand up like miniature mountains; the heat cracks the ground till it opens in crevices, sometimes a foot wide and a yard or two deep; fallen saplings lie hidden in the shadows to trip the horse, while the stumps stand up to cripple him, and over all is the long grass hiding all perils, and making the horse risk his own neck and his master's at every stride.

They flew along in the moonlight, Considine leading. Charlie next, then the two black boys, and then Carew, with a black gin on either side of him, racing in grim silence. The horses blundered and "pecked", stumbled, picked themselves up again, always seeming to have a leg to spare. Now and again a stump or a gaping crack in the ground would flash into view under their very nose, but they cleared everything—stumps, tussocks, gaps, and saplings.

In less time than it takes to write, they were between the mob and the scrub; at once a fusillade of whips rang out, and the men started to ride round the cattle in Indian file. The wild ones were well mixed up with the tame, and hardly knew which way to turn. Carew, cantering round, caught glimpses of them rushing hither and thither—small, wiry cattle for the most part, with big ears and sharp, spear-pointed horns. Of these there were fifty or sixty, as near as Considine could judge—three or four bulls, a crowd of cows and calves and half-grown animals, and a few old bullocks that had left the station mobs and thrown in their lot with the wild ones.

By degrees, as the horses went round them, the cattle began to "ring", forming themselves into a compact mass, those on the outside running round and round. All the time the whips were going, and the shrill cries of the blacks rang out, "Whoa back! Whoa back, there! Whoa!" as an animal attempted to break from the mob. They were gradually forcing the beasts away from the scrub, when suddenly, in spite of the gins' shrill cries, some of the leaders broke out and set off up the plain; with the rush of a cavalry charge the rest were after them, racing at full speed parallel with the edge of the scrub, and always trying to make over towards it.

Old Considine met this new development with Napoleonic quickness. He and the others formed a line parallel with the course of the cattle, and raced along between them and the timber, keeping up an incessant fusillade with their whips, while the old man's voice rang out loudly in directions to the blacks behind.

"Keep the coachers with 'em! Flog 'em along! Cut the hides off 'em!"

In the first rush the quiet cattle had dropped to the rear, but the blacks set about them with their whips; and, as they were experienced coachers, and had been flogged and hustled along in similar rushes so often that they knew at once what was wanted, they settled down to race just as fast as the wild ones. As the swaying, bellowing mass swept along in the moonlight, crashing and trampling through the light outlying timber, some of the coachers were seen working their way to the lead, and the wild cattle having no settled plan, followed them blindly. Considine, on his black horse, was close up by the wing of the mob, and the others rode in line behind him, always keeping between the cattle and the scrub.

"Crack your whips!" he yelled. "Crack your whips! Keep 'em off the scrub! Go on, Billy, drive that horse along and get to the lead!"

Like a flash one of the black boys darted out of the line, galloped to the head of the cattle, and rode there, pursued by the flying mob, the cracks of his heavy stockwhip sounding above the roar of hoofs and the bellowing of the cattle. Soon they steadied a little, and gradually sobered down till they stopped and began to "ring" again.

"That was pretty pure, eh, Mister?" roared Considine to Carew. "Ain't it a caution the way the coachers race with 'em? That old bald-face coacher is worth two men and a boy in a dash like this."

Suddenly an old bull, the patriarch of the wild herd, made towards one of the gins, whose shrill yells and whip-cracking failed to turn him. Considine dashed to her assistance, swinging his whip round his head.

"Whoa back, there! Whoa back, will you!" he shouted. The bull paused irresolute for a second, and half-turned back to the mob, but the sight or scent of his native scrub decided him. Dropping his head, he charged straight at Considine. So sudden was the attack that the stockhorse had barely time to spring aside; but, quick as it was, Considine's revolver was quicker. The bull passed – bang! went the revolver, and bang! bang! bang! again, as the horse raced alongside, Considine leaning over and firing into the bull's ribs at very short range.

The other cattle, dazed by the firing, did not attempt to follow, and at the fourth shot the bull wheeled to charge. He stood a moment in the moonlight, bold and defiant, then staggered a little and looked round as though to say, "What have you done to me?" Bang! went the revolver again; the animal lurched, plunged forward, sank on his knees, and fell over on his side, dead.

"There, you swab," said the old man, "that'll larn you to break another time." Then he took once more his place in the patrol round the mob. They circled and eddied and pushed, always staring angrily at the riders. Suddenly a big, red bullock gave a snort of defiance, and came out straight towards Carew. He stopped once, shook his head ominously, and came on again. One of the gins dashed up with the whip; but the bullock had evidently decided to take all chances, and advanced on his foes at a trot.

"Choot him, that feller!" screamed the gin to Carew. "You choot him! He bin yan away! No more stop! Choot him!"

Carew lugged out his revolver, and tried to pull his horse to a standstill, but the wary old veteran knew better than to be caught standing by a charging bullock; just as Carew fired, he plunged forward, with the result that the bullet went over the mob altogether, and very nearly winged Charlie, who was riding on the far side. Then the bullock charged in earnest; and Carew's horse, seeing that if he wished to save human life he must take matters into his own hands, made a bolt for it. Carew half-turned in the saddle, and fired twice, only making the black boys on the far side cower down on their horses' necks. Then the horse took complete charge, and made off for the scrub with the bullock after him, and every animal in the mob after the bullock.

Nothing in the world could have stopped them. Considine and Charlie raced in front, alongside Carew, cracking their whips and shouting; the blacks flogged the coachers up with the wild cattle; but they held on their way, plunged with a mighty crash into the thick timber, and were lost. No horseman could ride a hundred yards in that timber at night. Coachers and all were gone together, and the dispirited hunters gathered at the edge of the scrub and looked at each other.

"Well, Mister, you couldn't stop him," said the old man.

"I'm afraid I made—rather a mess of things, don't you know," said the Englishman. "I thought I hit him the second time, too. Seemed to be straight at him."

"I think you done very well to miss us! I heard one bullet whiz past me like a scorpyun. Well, it can't be helped. Those old coachers will all battle their way home again before long. Gordon, I vote we go home. They're your cattle now, and you'll have to come out again after 'em some day, and do a little more shootin'. Get a suit of armour on you first, though."

As they jogged home through the bright moonlight, they heard loud laughter from the blacks, and Carew, looking back, found the fat gin giving a dramatic rehearsal of his exploits. She dashed her horse along at a great pace, fell on his neck, clutched wildly at the reins, then suddenly turned in her saddle, and pretended to fire point-blank at the other blacks, who all dodged the bullet. Then she fell on the horse's neck again, and so on *ad lib*.

This made the Englishman very morose. He was quite glad when Charlie said he had seen enough of the cattle, and they would all start next day for civilisation—Charlie to resume the management of Mr Grant's stations, Carew to go with him as "colonial experiencer", and Considine to start for England to look after his inheritance.

Song of the Artesian Water

DECEMBER 1896

Now the stock have started dying, for the Lord has sent a drought;
But we're sick of prayers and Providence — we're going to do without;
With the derricks up above us and the solid earth below,
We are waiting at the lever for the word to let her to.
   Sinking down, deeper down,
     Oh, we'll sink it deeper down:
As the drill is plugging downward at a thousand feet of level,
If the Lord won't send us water, oh, we'll get it from the devil;
     Yes, we'll get it from the devil deeper down.

Now, our engine's built in Glasgow by a very canny Scot,
And he marked it twenty horsepower, but he don't know what is what:
When Canadian Bill is firing with the sun-dried gidgee logs,
She can equal thirty horses and a score or so of dogs.
   Sinking down, deeper down,
     Oh, we're going deeper down:
If we fail to get the water then it's ruin to the squatter,
For the drought is on the station and the weather's growing hotter,
     But we're bound to get the water deeper down.

But the shaft has started caving and the sinking's very slow,
And the yellow rods are bending in the water down below,
And the tubes are always jamming and they can't be made to shift
Till we nearly burst the engine with a forty horsepower lift.
   Sinking down, deeper down,
     Oh, we're going deeper down
Though the shaft is always caving, and the tubes are always jamming,
Yet we'll fight our way to water while the stubborn drill is ramming —
     While the stubborn drill is ramming deeper down.

But there's no artesian water, though we've passed three thousand feet,
And the contract price is growing and the boss is nearly beat.
But it must be down beneath us, and it's down we've got to go,
Though she's bumping on the solid rock four thousand feet below.
   Sinking down, deeper down,
     Oh, we're going deeper down:
And it's time they heard us knocking on the roof of Satan's dwellin';
But we'll get artesian water if we cave the roof of Hell in —
     Oh! we'll get artesian water deeper down.

But it's hark! the whistle's blowing with a wild, exultant blast,
And the boys are madly cheering, for they've struck the flow at last,
And it's rushing up the tubing from four thousand feet below
Till it spouts above the casing in a million-gallon flow.
   And it's down, deeper down —
     Oh, it comes from deeper down;
It is flowing, ever flowing, in a free, unstinted measure
From the silent hidden places where the old earth hides her treasure —
     Where the old earth hides her treasure deeper down.

And it's clear away the timber, and it's let the water run:
How it glimmers in the shadow, how it flashes in the sun!
By the silent belts of timber, by the miles of blazing plain
It is bringing hope and comfort to the thirsty land again.
   Flowing down, further down;
     It is flowing further down
To the tortured thirsty cattle, bringing gladness in its going;
Through the droughty days of summer it is flowing, ever flowing —
     It is flowing, ever flowing, further down.

DRILLING FOR WATER

BANJO PATERSON'S PEOPLE

SONG OF THE FUTURE

DECEMBER 1889

'Tis strange that in a land so strong,
So strong and bold in mighty youth,
We have no poet's voice of truth
To sing for us a wondrous song.

Our chiefest singer yet has sung
In wild, sweet notes a passing strain,
All carelessly and sadly flung
To that dull world he thought so vain.

"I care for nothing, good nor bad,
My hopes are gone, my pleasures fled,
I am but sifting sand," he said:
What wonder Gordon's songs were sad!

And yet, not always sad and hard;
In cheerful mood and light of heart
He told the tale of Britomarte,
And wrote the Rhyme of Joyous Guard.

And some have said that Nature's face
To us is always sad; but these
Have never felt the smiling grace
Of waving grass and forest trees
On sunlit plains as wide as seas.

"A land where dull Despair is king
O'er scentless flower and songless bird!"
But we have heard the bellbirds ring
Their silver bells at eventide,
Like fairies on the mountain side,
The sweetest note man ever heard.

The wild thrush lifts a note of mirth;
The bronzewing pigeons call and coo
Beside their nests the long day through;
The magpie warbles clear and strong
A joyous, glad, thanksgiving song,
For all God's mercies upon earth.

And many voices such as these
Are joyful sounds for those to tell,
Who know the Bush and love it well,
With all its hidden mysteries.

We cannot love the restless sea,
That rolls and tosses to and fro
Like some fierce creature in its glee;
For human weal or human woe
It has no touch of sympathy.

For us the bush is never sad:
Its myriad voices whisper low,
In tones the bushmen only know,
Its sympathy and welcome glad.

For us the roving breezes bring
From many a blossom-tufted tree—
Where wild bees murmur dreamily—
The honey-laden breath of Spring.

We have no tales of other days,
No bygone history to tell;
Our tales are told where campfires blaze
At midnight, when the solemn hush

Of that vast wonderland, the Bush,
Hath laid on every heart its spell.

Although we have no songs of strife,
Of bloodshed reddening the land,
We yet may find achievements grand
Within the bushman's quiet life.

Lift ye your faces to the sky
Ye far blue mountains of the west,
Who lie so peacefully at rest
Enshrouded in a haze of blue;
'Tis hard to feel that years went by
Before the pioneers broke through
Your rocky heights and walls of stone,
And made your secrets all their own.

For years the fertile western plains
Were hid behind your sullen walls,
Your cliffs and crags and waterfalls
All weatherworn with tropic rains.

Between the mountains and the sea,
Like Israelites with staff in hand,
The people waited restlessly:
They looked towards the mountains old
And saw the sunsets come and go
With gorgeous golden afterglow,
That made the west a fairyland,
And marvelled what that west might be
Of which such wondrous tales were told.

BANJO PATERSON'S PEOPLE

AUSTRALIA PAST AND FUTURE

For tales were told of inland seas
Like sullen oceans, salt and dead,
And sandy deserts, white and wan,
Where never trod the foot of man.

Nor bird went winging overhead,
Nor ever stirred a gracious breeze
To wake the silence with its breath—
A land of loneliness and death.

At length the hardy pioneers
By rock and crag found out the way,
And woke with voices of today,
A silence kept for years and years.

Upon the western slope they stood
And saw—a wide expanse of plain
As far as eye could stretch or see
Go rolling westward endlessly.
The native grasses, tall as grain,
Were waved and rippled in the breeze;
From boughs of blossom-laden trees
The parrots answered back again.
They saw the land that it was good,
A land of fatness all untrod,
And gave their silent thanks to God.

The way is won! The way is won!
And straightway from the barren coast
There came a westward-marching host,
That aye and ever onward prest
With eager faces to the west,
Along the pathway of the sun.

The mountains saw them marching by:
They faced the all-consuming drought,
They would not rest in settled land:

But, taking each his life in hand,
Their faces ever westward bent
Beyond the farthest settlement,
Responding to the challenge cry
Of "better country further out".

And lo a miracle! the land
But yesterday was all unknown,
The wild man's boomerang was thrown
Where now great busy cities stand.

It was not much, you say, that these
Should win their way where none
    withstood;
In sooth there was not much of blood
No war was fought between the seas.

It was not much! but we who know
The strange capricious land they trod—
At times a stricken, parching sod,
At times with raging floods beset—
Through which they found their lonely way,
Are quite content that you should say

It was not much, while we can feel
That nothing in the ages old,
In song or story written yet
On Grecian urn or Roman arch,
Though it should ring with clash of steel,
Could braver histories unfold
Than this bush story, yet untold—
The story of their westward march.

But times are changed, and changes rung
From old to new—the olden days,
The old bush life and all its ways
Are passing from us all unsung.

The freedom, and the hopeful sense
Of toil that brought due recompense,
Of room for all, has passed away,
And lies forgotten with the dead.
Within our streets men cry for bread
In cities built but yesterday.

About us stretches wealth of land,
A boundless wealth of virgin soil
As yet unfruitful and untilled!
Our willing workmen, strong and skilled
Within our cities idle stand,
And cry aloud for leave to toil.

The stunted children come and go
In squalid lanes and alleys black;
We follow but the beaten track
Of other nations, and we grow
In wealth for some—for many, woe.

And it may be that we who live
In this new land apart, beyond
The hard old world grown fierce
    and fond
And bound by precedent and bond,
May read the riddle right and give
New hope to those who dimly see
That all things may be yet for good,
And teach the world at length to be
One vast united brotherhood.

So may it be, and he who sings
In accents hopeful, clear, and strong,
The glories which that future brings
Shall sing, indeed, a wondrous song.

BANJO PATERSON'S PEOPLE

OLD PARDON, THE SON OF REPRIEVE

DECEMBER 1888

You never heard tell of the story?
   Well, now, I can hardly believe!
Never heard of the honour and glory
   Of Pardon, the son of Reprieve?
But maybe you're only a Johnnie
   And don't know a horse from a hoe?
Well, well, don't get angry, my sonny,
   But, really, a young 'un should know.

They bred him out back on the "Never",
   His mother was Mameluke breed.
To the front—and then stay there—was ever
   The root of the Mameluke creed.
He seemed to inherit their wiry
   Strong frames—and their pluck to receive—
As hard as a flint and as fiery
   Was Pardon, the son of Reprieve.

We ran him at many a meeting
   At crossing and gully and town,
And nothing could give him a beating—
   At least when our money was down.
For weight wouldn't stop him, nor distance,
   Nor odds, though the others were fast,
He'd race with a dogged persistence,
   And wear them all down at the last.

At the Turon the Yattendon filly
   Led by lengths at the mile and a half,
And we all began to look silly,
   While *her* crowd were starting to laugh;
But the old horse came faster and faster,
   His pluck told its tale, and his strength,
He gained on her, caught her, and passed her,
   And won it, hands down, by a length.

And then we swooped down on Menindie
   To run for the President's Cup—
Oh! that's a sweet township—a shindy
   To them is board, lodging, and sup.
Eye-openers they are, and their system
   Is never to suffer defeat;
It's "win, tie, or wrangle"—to best 'em
   You must lose 'em, or else it's "dead heat".

We strolled down the township and found 'em
   At drinking and gaming and play;
If sorrows they had, why they drowned 'em,
   And betting was soon under way.
Their horses were good 'uns and fit 'uns,
   There was plenty of cash in the town;
They backed their own horses like Britons,
   And Lord! how *we* rattled it down!

With gladness we thought of the morrow,
   We counted our wagers with glee,
A simile homely to borrow—
   "There was plenty of milk in our tea".
You see we were green; and we never
   Had even a thought of foul play,
Though we well might have known that the clever
   Division would "put us away".

Experience "*docet*", they tell us,
   At least so I've frequently heard,
But, "dosing" or "stuffing", those fellows
   Were up to each move on the board;
They got to his stall—it is sinful
   To think what such villains would do—
And they gave him a regular skinful
   Of barley—green barley—to chew.

He munched it all night, and we found him
   Next morning as full as a hog—
The girths wouldn't nearly meet round him;
   He looked like an overfed frog.
We saw we were done like a dinner—
   The odds were a thousand to one
Against Pardon turning up winner,
   'Twas cruel to ask him to run.

We got to the course with our troubles,
  A crestfallen couple were we;
And we heard the "books" calling the doubles—
  A roar like the surf of the sea;
And over the tumult and louder
  Rang, "Any price Pardon, I lay!"
Says Jimmy, "The children of Judah
  Are out on the warpath to-day."

Three miles in three heats: Ah, my sonny
  The horses in those days were stout,
They had to run well to win money;
  I don't see such horses about.
Your six-furlong vermin that scamper
  Half a mile with their featherweight up;
They wouldn't earn much of their damper
  In a race like the President's Cup.

The first heat was soon set a-going;
  The Dancer went off to the front;
The Don on his quarters was showing,
  With Pardon right out of the hunt.
He rolled and he weltered and wallowed—
  You'd kick your hat faster, I'll bet;
They finished all bunched, and he followed
  All lathered and dripping with sweat.

But troubles came thicker upon us,
  For while we were rubbing him dry
The stewards came over to warn us:
  "We hear you are running a bye!
If Pardon don't spiel like tarnation
  And win the next heat—if he can—
He'll earn a disqualification;
  Just think over *that*, now, my man!"

Our money all gone and our credit,
  Our horse couldn't gallop a yard;
And then people thought that *we* did it!
  It really was terribly hard.
We were objects of mirth and derision
  To folk in the lawn and the stand,
And the yells of the clever division
  Of "Any price, Pardon!" were grand.

We still had a chance for the money,
  Two heats still remained to be run;
If both fell to us—why, my sonny,
  The clever division were done.
And Pardon was better, we reckoned,
  His sickness was passing away,
So he went to the post for the second
  And principal heat of the day.

They're off and away with a rattle,
  Like dogs from the leashes let slip,
And right at the back of the battle
  He followed them under the whip.
They gained ten good lengths on him quickly,
  He dropped right away from the pack;
I tell you it made me feel sickly
  To see the blue jacket fall back.

Our very last hope had departed—
  We thought the old fellow was done,
When all of a sudden he started
  To go like a shot from a gun.
His chances seemed slight to embolden
  Our hearts; but, with teeth firmly set,
We thought, "Now or never! The old 'un
  May reckon with some of 'em yet,"

Then loud rose the warcry for Pardon;
  He swept like the wind down the dip,
And over the rise by the garden,
  The jockey was done with the whip;
The field were at sixes and sevens—
  The pace at the first had been fast—
And hope seemed to drop from the heavens,
  For Pardon was coming at last.

BANJO PATERSON'S PEOPLE

THE HEREAFTER RACECOURSE

BANJO PATERSON'S PEOPLE

And how he did come! It was splendid;
  He gained on them yards every bound,
Stretching out like a greyhound extended,
  His girth laid right down on the ground.
A shimmer of silk in the cedars
  As into the running they wheeled,
And out flashed the whips on the leaders,
  For Pardon had collared the field.

Then right through the ruck he came sailing—
  I knew that the battle was won—
The son of Haphazard was failing,
  The Yattendon filly was done;
He cut down the Don and the Dancer,
  He raced clean away from the mare—
He's in front! Catch him now if you can, sir!
  And up went my hat in the air!

Then loud from the lawn and the garden
  Rose offers of "Ten to one *on*!"
"Who'll bet on the field? I back Pardon!"
  No use; all the money was gone.
He came for the third heat light-hearted,
  A-jumping and dancing about;
The others were done ere they started
  Crestfallen, and tired, and worn out.

He won it, and ran it much faster
  Than even the first, I believe
Oh, he was the daddy, the master,
  Was Pardon, the son of Reprieve.
He showed 'em the method to travel—
  The boy sat as still as a stone—
They never could see him for gravel;
  He came in hard-held, and alone.

But he's old—and his eyes are grown hollow;
  Like me, with my thatch of the snow;
When he dies, then I hope I may follow,
  And go where the racehorses go,
I don't want no harping nor singing—
  Such things with my style don't agree;
Where the hoofs of the horses are ringing
  There's music sufficient for me.

And surely the thoroughbred horses
  Will rise up again and begin
Fresh races on faraway courses
  And p'raps they might let me slip in.
It would look rather well the race card on
  'Mongst cherubs and seraphs and things,
"Angel Harrison's black gelding Pardon,
  Blue halo, white body and wings".

And if they have racing hereafter,
  (And who is to say they will not?)
When the cheers and the shouting and laughter
  Proclaim that the battle grows hot;
As they come down the racecourse a-steering,
  He'll rush to the front, I believe;
And you'll hear the great multitude cheering
  For Pardon, the son of Reprieve.